Palgrave Macmillan Studies in Banking and Financial Institutions

Series Editor
Philip Molyneux
University of Sharjah
Sharjah, United Arab Emirates

The Palgrave Macmillan Studies in Banking and Financial Institutions series is international in orientation and includes studies of banking systems in particular countries or regions as well as contemporary themes such as Islamic Banking, Financial Exclusion, Mergers and Acquisitions, Risk Management, and IT in Banking. The books focus on research and practice and include up to date and innovative studies that cover issues which impact banking systems globally.

More information about this series at
http://www.palgrave.com/gp/series/14678

Mariarosa Borroni • Simone Rossi

Banking in Europe

The Quest for Profitability after the Great Financial Crisis

palgrave
macmillan

Mariarosa Borroni
Department of Economics and Social Sciences
Università Cattolica del Sacro Cuore
Piacenza, Piacenza, Italy

Simone Rossi
Department of Economics and Social Sciences
Università Cattolica del Sacro Cuore
Piacenza, Piacenza, Italy

ISSN 2523-336X ISSN 2523-3378 (electronic)
Palgrave Macmillan Studies in Banking and Financial Institutions
ISBN 978-3-030-15012-9 ISBN 978-3-030-15013-6 (eBook)
https://doi.org/10.1007/978-3-030-15013-6

Cover illustration: fanjianhua / Getty Images

This Palgrave Pivot imprint is published by the registered company Springer Nature Switzerland AG.
The registered company address is: Gewerbestrasse 11, 6330 Cham, Switzerland

Acknowledgements

We are thankful to Philip Molyneux, series editor for Studies in Banking and Financial Institutions, for the opportunity to publish this volume, and to the staff at Palgrave Macmillan, especially Ruth Noble and Tula Weis, for helpful guidance. Furthermore, we would like to thank our colleagues/ friends and two anonymous reviewers for their helpful comments. Any errors are our own.

Introduction

Profitability is a crucial goal for a firm; it is very likely to be the most important one. This statement holds for several kinds of enterprises, operating in different sectors. Although it can be criticized, for example, with reference to specific institutions operating under a mutualistic approach to the market, it is widely accepted within modern economies. Making a profit means that a firm is able to generate a stream of revenue that is greater than its operating costs, and in a broad sense, it signals the success of the firm within the market. Not surprisingly, this leads to the commonly held belief that states that a profitable firm is usually also a sound enterprise.

Over time, several elements contribute to the shape of profitability of a specific business: the level of interest rates, inflation, general economic growth, competition within the sector and so forth. Profitability is usually pro-cyclical, in that during economic downturns, the level of profits falls sharply, and some firms default, exiting the market for ever. The knock-on effects of these events influence the whole economy and are typically stronger when the defaulting institution is systemically important due to its dimension or function. In this respect, the banking sector plays a crucial role within the economy of a country, and it is not surprising that its profitability is a strong indicator of the health of a specific economic and financial system.

In many ways banks represent a fundamental pillar sustaining modern economies, and they are active both in direct and in indirect finance. Deterioration of the surrounding environment leads to a worse asset quality and lower revenues for the banking system. The main problem here is that banks are at the same time the target and the promoters of the dynamics of the economic cycle; they are—as it is usually expressed—'systemically important'. While in recent times, this notion has assumed a specific regulatory meaning (as we will see later in more detail), more informally we agree with the idea that a bank default can exert a strong negative impact on a specific territory (be this large or small, it does not matter). Given that banks represent a transmission channel for transferring purchasing power within the economy, their default can be at the same time the effect of defaulting firms and the cause of economic downturns; they can transform a crisis at a microeconomic level into one at a macroeconomic level. This is the reason why the health of the banking system is a key issue for policymakers and regulators and, at the same time, it explains the enormous output of prudential regulation over time.

The severe crisis that started in the US in mid-2007 has had intense and long-lasting effects on the banking sector; one of the most important—and easily observed—results of this troubled period has been a dramatic fall in bank profitability. This outcome is particularly dangerous for the financial industry and so for the whole economy, in that the resilience of a bank depends on its level of regulatory capital, and its ability to increase this aggregate is strongly linked to the remuneration offered to its shareholders. Moreover, recent prudential regulation has strengthened the importance of self-financing as a measure for reinforcing the level of capital ratio. Hence, reestablishing a sound level of profitability has become a key point on the agendas of bankers, regulators and policymakers; in this area, some elements need to be managed and clarified.

On the one hand, from a technical point of view, it is necessary to define what we mean by profitability and which indicators we can use to measure it. In effect, over the years, different ratios have been used to define the profitability level of a specific firm; this has been particularly true for the banking system, which has peculiar features in terms of financial statements and business lines. These ratios can involve measures of profitability, profit volatility, risk-adjusted performance measures and others linked to financial market data; moreover, attention can be focused on the revenues of a specific business, as in the case of the interest margin. The possible combinations in this field are almost infinite.

On the other hand, from a strategic and managerial point of view, it is necessary to clarify how the profitability of a specific bank can be enhanced. This involves the ability of a firm to understand and anticipate the changes in the surrounding environment, choosing between the alternatives available at specific times. Internal development or outsourcing? Focusing or diversification? Innovation: friend or foe? These are a few of the questions that each year a bank's decision-makers need to face. Their ability to create a stable stream of profits is strongly correlated to their ability to find the right answers to these issues. The same holds for regulators and policy-makers, who can reshape the regulatory framework in which banks operate, promoting or reducing profit opportunities.

This book aims at providing a comprehensive overview of the preceding issues, examining the dynamics that have been affecting the profitability of European banks since the recent crisis period. More specifically, we shed light on the most crucial changes in profit generation and on the changes in banking strategies deriving from fiercer competition, reduced margins and changing regulation. The scope of the book is to provide a straightforward interpretative system for understanding and managing the continuous changes in the financial environment. The work is divided in four main parts. In the first one, we provide an overview of the changes in the technological, competitive, regulatory and macroeconomic context that affected the banking sector over the years of the great international financial crisis. In the second, we review the literature on bank profitability and outline the main determinants of profit generation. In the third, we provide a cross-country analysis of profitability for a wide sample of European banks; this includes panel regressions and cluster analysis both on profitability and risk-adjusted performance measures. In the last section of the book, we discuss the results of this quantitative analysis in the light of the new regulatory and competitive framework (Banking Union, fintech, Basel regulation, etc.) that is progressively affecting the banking sector.

Contents

List of Figures

List of Tables

CHAPTER 1

Bank Management After the Great Crisis

Abstract This chapter provides an overview of the changes in the technological, competitive, regulatory and macroeconomic context that affected the banking sector over the years of the great international financial crisis. In particular, the dynamics linked to the entry into the market of new (and innovative) competitors, the opportunities deriving from the reshaping of the business model and the delicate balance between efficiency and competitiveness on the market are considered; the topic of the new rules affecting the banking sector in Europe is also critically examined.

Keywords SREP • Regulation • Fintech • Non-performing loans (NPLs) • Price-to-book value • Financial crisis

1.1 Introduction

There have been many structural changes that have affected the banking system since the long financial crisis: a very changeable economic context, increasingly pervasive intervention of the supervisory authorities, a serious economic recession whose 'creeping' effects are still noticeable in many countries, the tumultuous development of technological innovation, the adoption of unconventional monetary policy instruments and the continuation of low,

M. Borroni, S. Rossi, *Banking in Europe*, Palgrave Macmillan Studies in Banking and Financial Institutions,
https://doi.org/10.1007/978-3-030-15013-6_1

when not negative, interest rates. All this has been reflected in the way banking has been carried on; it is experiencing substantial changes, perhaps as never before in any previous period. One of the most important consequences, at least in Europe, is represented by a persistent period of weak profitability which, for many credit institutions in recent years, has often resulted in even negative rates of profit. Since it is well known that a prolonged absence of profitability generates negative consequences on the soundness of banks and on the stability of the entire credit sector, scholars, practitioners and supervisory authorities have developed a (new) line of investigation regarding the strategic and operational choices of banks and, as a consequence, their organizational structures, that is their business model.

1.2 Bank Business Model: What Has Been Changing in the Fintech Era

The prevailing business model of the European banking sector, naturally widely influenced by the structure of the economic system whose financial needs it is destined to meet, is that of traditional commercial retail banking, that is, a banking system with a strong incidence of lending activity on total assets, and funding made up largely of deposits channeled through a wide-reaching and widespread local branch network. There is certainly no shortage of significant and important examples of investment banks designed to satisfy the most complex financial needs, located in the main financial centers and operating on a global scale; however, the core component of the European credit system is as summarized above.

The crisis in the banking system, which has lasted for a significant period, has led to a rethinking of banks' business models. The sustainability of banking strategies has become a source of concern for regulators, especially in the euro area, such as to induce them to include a careful examination of the business model adopted by each bank intermediary in the Supervisory Priorities (https://www.bankingsupervision.europa.eu/banking/priorities) and in the Supervisory Review and Evaluation Process (SREP) of each individual credit institution (i.e. the regular evaluation exercise performed by the regulatory authorities for the measurement of risks at the individual bank level and the definition of any actions to be taken).

As we will see in the course of this work, there is no one model clearly superior to the others; the various surveys carried out and reported in the literature and in the regulatory field show a great variety of results (ECB Banking Supervision, 2018), even when the business model is changed

(Roengpitya et al., 2017; Ayadi et al., 2018). What everyone seems to agree on is the role in the coming years that technology will have on the redefinition of the business model, and on all banking activity in general.

One of the great challenges facing banks in coming years, and which in many contexts is already a significant issue, is financial technology, or fintech. This term is used to refer to very diverse activities and players sharing some specific features: a marked/exclusive use of technology for carrying out various forms of financial activity, intermediaries' adoption of new business models and the creation, or rather the re-adaptation, of financial instruments and/or services that, by virtue of this technology, guarantee greater security, speed of execution and lower costs, and can be offered to a wider range of users (FSB, 2017). Fintech companies offer competing products and services in many of the key business areas of traditional brick-and-mortar intermediaries (payments, lending, trading, asset management). Fintech has now gone well beyond being just a buzzword or a niche area for young nerds: investments in the first half of 2018 have surpassed those made in the previous year, exceeding 40 billion US dollars (source: FinTech Global); in 2018, the venture capital sector alone financed fintech deals for over 50 billion US dollars (source: IMF, 2018). Furthermore, besides the fintech companies themselves, growing importance is accruing to the so-called BigTech firms: GAFA (acronym for Google, Apple, Facebook and Amazon; or Alibaba, especially for Asiatic areas) have redefined customer experience across all sectors, including financial services, as they leverage new technologies, sizeable volumes of data and actionable insights to both understand and predict customers' behaviors and needs.

The debate which developed at the beginning of the decade has seen the emergence of two opposing positions with regard to the possible evolution of digital banking: on the one hand, there are those who advocate totally disruptive scenarios for the banking system, even hypothesizing the end of banks (in agreement with the famous statement by Bill Gates, 1994, "Banking is necessary, banks are not"); on the other hand, there are those who believe that the fintech phenomenon, like so many others, is destined to 'deflate' in a few years ("fintech is only another bubble"), as soon as events with significant negative consequences occur in the sector. Without any exaggeration, it is undoubtedly true that the phenomenon represents a significant change in the way banking is perceived: technology, now so pervasive in everyday life, has profoundly changed both users' and producers', banks' and other financial intermediaries' approach in the financial field too. The huge challenge that banks are facing is therefore to comprehend whether they are still called upon to play a fundamental role in all segments of financial intermediation, or whether, in some way or for certain areas of activity, other operators will progressively replace them, to a greater or lesser degree. Millennials (young people in their teens to mid-30s) are emblematic in this respect: over half do not see any difference between their bank and others, and would be much more interested in a new financial service offered by Google or Apple than one provided by their bank (Chishti and Barberis, 2016).

Dermine (2016) outlines three main areas in which banking activity could be hit, to a greater or lesser degree, by the development of digital technology: the first is the payment system and brokerage of financial instruments (including passively managed mutual investment funds). In this case, the required expertise involves data processing and not banking business in the strict sense: this explains the attractiveness of the segment for large operators accustomed to processing huge amounts of data, at ever-increasing rates and with very low costs. The newcomers in the payment business (PayPal, Apple, etc.) and the transfer of funds at international level (TransferWise), and their increasing market shares, well exemplify the importance of this threat.

The second area of interest for financial technology consists in those banking products and services that require data analysis and some banking expertise, though not particularly sophisticated: for example, forms of consumer credit or low loan-to-value mortgages, or the management of savings of relatively limited assets. The work done by the credit officer or financial advisor can be handled, in the first case, by electronic (online) platforms, not necessarily operated by commercial banks, that match borrowers with lenders (peer-to-peer lending, loan-based crowdfunding, marketplace lending), and use algorithms and big data to provide a risk ranking for screen borrowers; in the second case by robot-advisor services, a cheap alternative to 'traditional' human wealth advisors. In both cases, in contrast with what happens in a traditional bank, the typical feature of a fintech company is that it makes use of digital technologies and innovations to interact fully (or largely) with online customers and processes large amounts of information (Panetta, 2018; Claessens et al., 2018).

Finally, there is a third area where banks are much more difficult to supplant with a fintech entity and which is typical of any credit institution, that is, its funding and lending activity and its ability to solve mismatch maturities. On the one hand, banks guarantee liquidity and certain repayment of the sums deposited, thanks to the presence of public or private insurance schemes; on the other hand, they always make credit available to borrowers, especially for higher risk transactions in which information—especially 'soft' type difficult to process using technological algorithms—plays an important role in decision-making.

The development of fintech is unstoppable, and in many ways may also be beneficial: it has recently been demonstrated that although digital technology alone is not able to increase financial inclusion, nonetheless, "the use of financial technology, including the use of mobile phones and the internet to conduct financial transactions, may be expanded to include people who do not have an account—the unbanked—as well as to promote greater use of digital financial services among those who do have an account" (Demirgüç-Kunt et al., 2018).

It is also unavoidable that fintech will tread on banks' toes: the inevitable consequence, for the latter, is a progressive reduction of their market power in traditional business, with a consequent significant reduction in profit margins: recent surveys have reported that bankers estimate they will lose a quarter of their market share due to further development of fintech, and that the expansion of fintech firms could erode 60% of banks' retail services profits (McKinsey, 2017).

In Europe, the first major challenge has already been launched by the enforcement of Payment Services Directive 2 (PSD2; EU 2015/2366), which aims to develop a single integrated payment market, standardizing the rules between payment service providers and contributing to strengthening the security of the system, as well as ensuring a high level of competition and transparency toward consumers. In fact, PSD2 introduces, for those who use an online current account, the possibility of making payments (Payment Initiation Services: PIS) or accessing bank account information (Account Information Services: AIS) through software created by authorized third parties (Third Party Providers: TPPs). Banks are required to set up dedicated interfaces to communicate with TPPs; the new players, if authorized, will be able to operate on the current accounts of end users. If on the one hand this possibility determines a serious risk of disintermediation for the traditional bank (incumbent), together with a potential loss of competent personnel, attracted by more innovative operating sectors, on the other it opens new opportunities for the development of increasingly innovative and efficient services for customers. At the regulatory level, this determines an important consequence. It is in fact the responsibility of the authorities to create a 'level playing field': regulation should be concerned with the service provided, rather than with who is providing (Fig. 1.1).

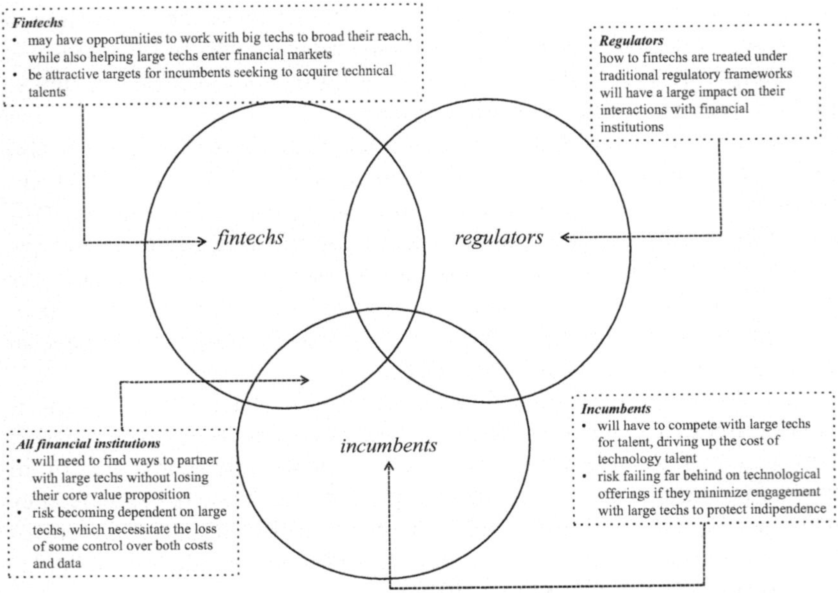

Fig. 1.1 The impact of fintech on the financial system. Source: World Economic Forum (2017)

1.3 Regulatory Framework: Opportunities and Threats for the Banking System

The financial system is a fundamental infrastructure in any modern economic system, and the stability of the intermediaries operating in it is the main, though not exclusive, objective of all regulatory and control authorities. The question is not *if* banking should be regulated, but *to what extent*, and how pervasive regulation should be. The memory of the bank failures that characterized the beginning of last century, and the terrible long-term consequences for the entire international economic system, are fresh in the memory of any regulator. The numerous actions put in place by policymakers since the bankruptcy of Lehman Brothers in September 2008 are thus justified; the objective was to 'secure' the system, to avoid bank runs and to limit, as much as possible, the systemic consequences that may be caused by the insolvency of banking intermediaries.

This is not the place to retrace the long series of regulatory measures that have been introduced over the last decade; however, it has certainly involved a real reregulation of banking, following several decades of thorough deregulation. "This time is different": on the basis of this presumed contrast with the past, during the final decade of the last century, a regulatory apparatus that could perhaps at least have limited the problems arising from the long financial crisis that was then experienced, was progressively dismantled and, in some cases, completely eliminated. Reinhart and Rogoff (2009) recall how history shows that very little is learned from mistakes made in the past: the ability of governments and investors to "deceive themselves", giving rise to attacks of irrational euphoria that usually result in heavy and prolonged periods of wealth destruction, seems to remain unchanged. What made the impact of the recent crisis more devastating has been the strong degree of interconnection between the various economic systems, made possible partly by technological progress. The insolvency of one intermediary, even if not 'too big', becomes a problem at the international level, precisely because of the systemic fallout that can derive from it, and it is increasingly difficult to stem the consequences.

Over the last decade, during the first phase, regulatory actions were almost emergency measures with the main objective of strengthening the assets of credit institutions, in the belief that a high endowment of own funds reduces banks' propensity to risk-taking, increases resistance in situations of sudden crises and guarantees macroeconomic stability. There are two main factors that determined the vulnerability of the international banking system: an excessive level of leverage and limited stable sources of funding. The difficulties, initially limited to the US subprime markets, quickly turned into a global crisis and, in many cases, forced the public sector to intervene. Although the crisis originated overseas, the greatest and heaviest consequences in terms of losses mainly occurred in the European banking sector (on this point see also Chap. 3).

The regulatory reforms launched in the aftermath of the outbreak of the crisis, mainly summarized in the review of the rules contained in the so-called Basel Accords (Basel III), have now mostly been finalized (BCBS, 2017). The new rules have adopted a two-step approach. Firstly, as of 2010, the focus has been on increasing the size and quality of banks' capital assets, as well as on strengthening risk-weighted capital requirements (RWCR) through restrictions on capital and liquidity. This first phase, now mostly completed (Table 1.1), has led to a sharp increase in the levels of bank assets, thus permitting the stemming of new systemic crises and guaranteeing banks a return to normal operations.

Table 1.1 Basel III key standards

Standard	*Adoption year*	*Requirement*	*Phase-in from year*	*Full implementation year*
Stage 1: Capital and liquidity				
Capital definition	2010	CET1; deductions	2013	2022
Minimum CET1 ratio	2010	4.5%	2013	2015
Capital conservation buffer	2010	2.5%	2016	2019
Countercyclical buffer	2010	0–2.5%	2016	2019
G-SIB capital surcharge	2010	0–3.5%	2016	2019
Leverage ratio (LR)	2010	3%	2015 (disclosure)	2018
Securitization framework	*2014*	*Revised framework*		*2018*
Market risk framework	*2016*	*Revised framework*		*2022*
Liquidity coverage ratio	2010	100%	2015	2019
Net stable funding ratio	2010	100%		2018
Stage 2: Tackling RWA variability				
Output floor	2017	72.5%	2022	2027
LR revisions/G-SIB surcharge	2017	50% scaling factor		2022
Credit risk framework	2017	Revised framework		2022
Operational risk framework	2017	Revised framework		2022

Source: BIS (2018). The Basel framework distinguishes three pillars: (1) minimum capital requirements; (2) supervisory review and (3) market discipline, based on standardized disclosures. Complementary reforms, such as enhanced bank resolution regimes, are implemented in parallel

During the second stage, focus centered on the comparability and reliability of the internal models used to calculate RWCRs, which allow banks to calculate their own risk weightings. The use of internal models may give rise to significant variability in RWCR calculations, which the measures in question seek to limit in order to avoid situations of serious competitive disparity, as well as new sources of potential systemic risk. For this reason, some constraints have been set (input and output floor) which are particularly important in cases where the model presents a fairly high risk, due to lack of data or unverified or weakly robust modeling techniques.

The Basel III standards, introduced gradually over an extended time frame to facilitate banks in their progressive adjustment, are now in a generally advanced stage; the requirements of phase 1 are now operational almost everywhere, often ahead of the deadlines originally set by the Accord. Banks have adjusted their balance sheets to the new standards because of the pressure exerted by market expectations; fully loaded requirements have indeed become the benchmark for investors, and credit institutions, which are weak in regulatory terms, often suffer negative market valuations. Furthermore, the increasing use of stress tests by the supervisory authorities to assess the degree of resistance to sudden systemic shocks on the basis of fully loaded regulatory parameters has, in fact, 'obliged' banks to make early adjustment as regards the deadlines of the next phases.

The impact of the reforms is therefore evident: in the aggregate balance sheets of the Global Systemically Important Banks (G-SIBs), a greater quantity and a better quality of own funds (Fig. 1.2, left-hand panel), less dependence on short-term wholesale deposits and a greater quantity of high-quality liquid assets as well as a gradual move away from business lines linked to trading and a clearer shift toward a retail business model with relatively stable sources of funding (Fig. 1.2, central and right-hand panels) can be observed (CGFS, 2018). In particular, European Union banks have progressively and significantly strengthened their capital position, with

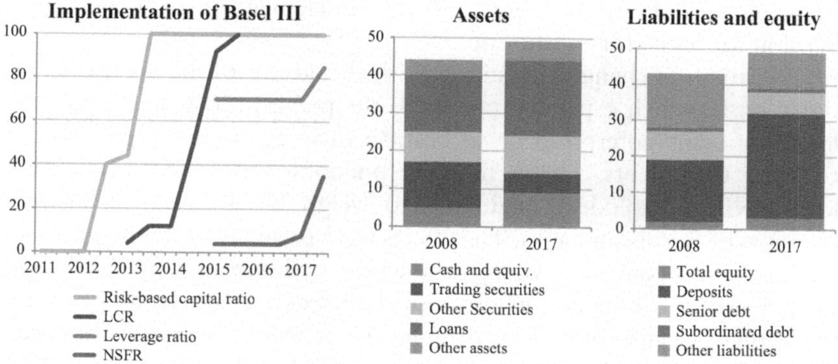

Fig. 1.2 Implementation of new requirements and adjustments for banks. Source: Adapted from BIS (2018). Implementation of Basel III figure: percentage of BCBS member jurisdictions in which each standard is in force. Asset and liabilities data: figures based on a balanced sample of 28 G-SIBs (trillions USD)

continuously increasing capital ratios which have now reached the highest levels since the beginning of the crisis (EBA, 2017).

If the emergency phase can therefore be considered reasonably concluded with the 'securing' of credit institutions, achieved through the continuous strengthening of levels of capitalization, important structural challenges nonetheless remain for banks, which continue to be characterized by weak profitability levels. This inability to generate profits from ordinary activities, or at any rate only producing them at very low levels, has become the main source of concern for regulatory authorities.

In the precrisis years, bank profitability was considered a purely academic research topic; the ability to generate income, often significantly higher than that of other economic sectors, allowed banks to cover production costs adequately, remunerate the invested capital to a satisfactory extent and, for this reason, attract new capital to implement development plans or comply with regulatory requirements. The limited manifestation of generalized crisis phenomena in Europe (Detken and Peltonen, 2017), especially when compared with what happened in the United States (on this, see the database maintained by the Federal Deposit Insurance Corporation—https://www.fdic.gov/bank/individual/failed/banklist.html), guaranteed some 'security' for investments in the banking sector which, together with a constant though not particularly significant growth rate, was received favorably by investors; a large share of portfolio value was in fact represented by securities in the banking and financial sector. This context did not therefore constitute an element of particular apprehension for regulatory authorities.

The situation changed drastically with the advent of the great international crisis, which expanded rapidly to the real economy, leading to the failure of many enterprises or, at best, to their experiencing difficulty in repaying their debts. This is how the phenomenon of non-performing loans (NPLs) exploded, beginning to weigh heavily on the financial accounts of European banks. The effects were naturally more disruptive in bank-oriented countries where production is dominated by small- and medium-sized companies, whose financial needs are largely, if not exclusively, met by bank credit. This complex macroeconomic context has been further exacerbated by the sovereign debt crisis for those countries (above all Italy and Greece) with a high public debt-to-GDP ratio. The significant presence of public debt securities on banks' balance sheets, together with the fear that the sovereign state will become insolvent, drastically reduces the value of the securities, obliging the banks to provide for write-downs and provisions, with obvious further negative repercussions on the income statement. To this can be added the fact that the impossibility of reliably outlining a general and consolidated economic recovery obliged the monetary authorities to keep interest rates at very low levels ("below zero rates"), and this phenomenon put additional pressures on bank profitability, further squeezing the net interest margin which is the main profit component, especially for retail banks.

In the second part of the decade, the relative improvement in the macroeconomic context generated beneficial effects on bank profitability, though not sufficiently so. A continued high stock of NPLs, a low level of cost efficiency and the sustainability of the business model amid a more competitive environment are key challenges for the European banking sector. The finalization of Basel III cannot therefore be considered an 'endgame' in regulatory terms; despite the progress made, market valuations (expressed through the price-to-book ratio; IMF, 2018) of many banks, in particular European banks, indicate a certain skepticism on the part of investors regarding income prospects, on which weigh the impact of legacy-related costs and uncertainties regarding business model sustainability.

There is another structural challenge facing the European banking system: overbanking. The European Systemic Risk Board has used this term to describe excessive growth in the European banking system ("rapid growth in bank size", "high concentration" and "high leverage among the largest banks"). Such a situation highlights at least two intrinsic dangers: the first is linked to the growth of the real economy, which could be compromised by the difficulties of the large banks that finance it; the second concerns the possibility that banks will become 'too big to save' in the event of a crisis, thus increasing the likelihood of further financial and sovereign crises, if the states were called on to intervene (ESRB, 2014). Similar considerations have been expressed by the ECB (Constancio, 2017) and by the IMF (IMF, 2017); an overbanking situation compresses the prices and margins charged by banks to companies, especially in highly competitive situations with reduced lending opportunities, and also affects costs and operational efficiency due to the high number of branches and employees, a situation that still distinguishes many European countries. It is true that both competitive pressure and labor market rigidities can inhibit the ability of, or incentive to, banks to restructure more quickly and aggressively; demographic factors can also influence the decision to maintain 'brick-and-mortar' branches, because older populations tend to prefer in-person rather than distance (mobile, internet) forms of banking. Moreover, it has been observed that branch network rationalization and headcount reductions have brought efficiency gains (traditionally measured through the reduction of the cost income ratio) in some, but not most, euro area banking sectors (Constancio, 2016).

Finally, as already mentioned above, there is another important challenge facing banks on the one hand and regulatory authorities on the other. For the former, rapid technological changes in the financial sector (various forms of 'fintech' innovations) can permit exploitation of economies of scale and consequently reduce costs. At the same time, however, these innovations favor the entry into the market of large BigTech players, which is typically unregulated since they do not belong to the financial sector. Their analytical skills, state-of-the-art technological infrastructures and a loyal customer base represent a real threat to banks, especially in the income field. The supervisory authorities thus have the difficult task of 'isolating' the financial component of these players' activity, and submitting it to rules similar to those envisaged for credit institutions, so as not to create situations of competitive disparity.

A decade has passed since the global financial crisis, and much progress has been made, but the regulators' to-do list is far from fulfillment. New international standards, better guidelines and best practices have been achieved, but at the same time the emergence of new risks and a certain legislative 'weariness', linked to continuous and pressing changes in the regulatory sphere, could undermine the progress made in recent years toward improving the stability of credit institutions. It must be borne in mind that no regulatory framework, even the most complete, can ever eliminate the probability of a crisis; risks arise and grow in positive periods, when a degree of euphoria due to the good performance of the economy leads to their underestimation. The regulatory framework is therefore far from complete, and the costs of this continuous regulatory adaptation will continue to weigh on bank profit margins for a long time.

1.4 Financial and Economic Environment: Surviving Squeezed Margins

Over the last decade, credit institutions have experienced one of the strongest contractions ever in their degree of profitability, albeit in very different ways from country to country and from bank to bank. In many cases, profitability has remained strongly negative for a number of years, leading to many operators exiting the market. The prolonged period of crisis that has engulfed the world economy, though involving differing time frames and degrees of intensity, has been the main cause of this dramatic reduction. Geopolitical factors and weak economic growth, if not true recession, have given rise to long periods of very low levels of inflation, low interest rates and extraordinary monetary policy intervention aimed at providing the market with the liquidity necessary to allow the economy to resume a virtuous path of development. As previously stated, at the European level, the situation has been rendered even more problematic by the onset of the sovereign debt crisis, especially in southern European countries where high levels of public debt—widely held by credit institutions operating internationally—and doubts about its repayment, or in some cases default, have further cast a negative shadow on the solvency of many banks.

Accurate and thorough identification of all the factors that have contributed to the dramatic drop in profitability experienced by the European banking system is not easy. Furthermore, different levels of interaction between these factors often depend partly on national specificities. Indeed, it should not be forgotten that the outbreak of the crisis occurred when the European banking system was united in a single currency but still largely fragmented at national level as regards the system of rules and controls on credit institutions. Figure 1.3 identifies the main elements, at least with regard to European banks, that have determined this sharp decline in profitability, albeit with varying degrees of relevance and impact in the different national contexts. As an example, regulatory guidelines on NPLs were not harmonized in all jurisdictions; this gave rise to (sometimes very evident) differences in their identification and measurement and in provisioning activity, as well as in the definition of the relevant prudential regulations (FSI, 2018).

Credit institutions, like all business categories, also suffered heavily in terms of performance from the difficult macroeconomic context in which they were operating. Poor growth prospects reduce or cancel investment, and as a result, fewer loans are disbursed by banks; lower interest income due to a reduced volume of loans can be offset by assuming a greater degree of risk, but this increases the probability of loan deterioration due borrower insolvency (NPLs), and therefore loan loss provisions, as well as all the related costs (legal fees, enforcement of guarantees, etc.). The more

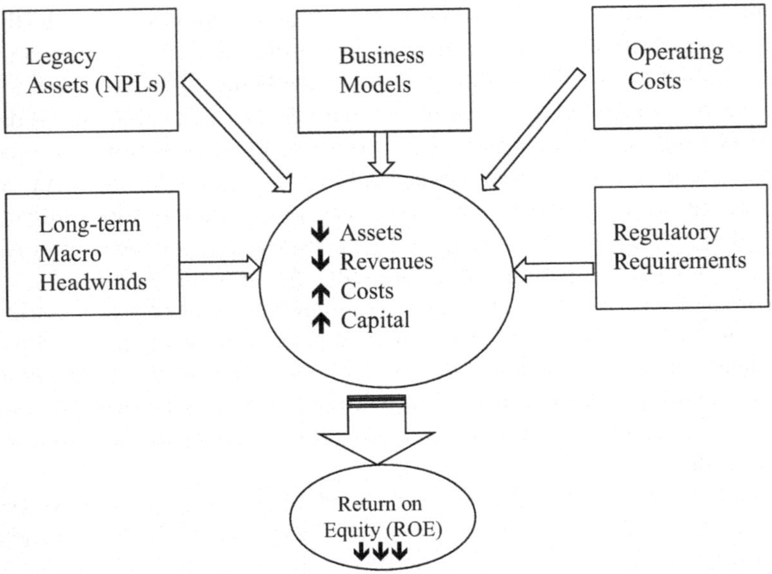

Fig. 1.3 Main factors affecting bank profitability. Source: Adapted from Jobst-Weber (2016)

an economic system is bank-oriented as regards financial resources for development, the more this phenomenon is accentuated, and heavy reliance on bank credit, especially by small- and medium-sized companies, and the resulting predominance in many banking systems of a lending-based business model has exacerbated the economic and financial difficulties of numerous credit institutions (at the end of 2016, loans comprised the most important position in almost all banking sectors; source: ECB, 2017). These difficulties led to solvency crises, in some cases resolved through injections of public capital, in others with the resolution of the bank itself by the supervisory authorities (the United Kingdom and Germany are among the first European countries where a systemic crisis materialized; ESRB, 2017).

Bank profit margins, and in particular the net interest margin, the main source of income for traditional commercial banks, have therefore been heavily compressed, due both to lower revenues (from interest) generated by reduced lending activity and an increase in funding costs, necessary to guarantee an adequate level of liquidity and comply with increasingly pressing regulatory requirements. A growing climate of distrust has encouraged institutional investors to demand a higher risk premium from credit institutions; account holders, in turn, alarmed by the banking crises, reduce their traditional contribution in the form of deposits—on which they receive almost zero rate interest—for fear of non-repayment.

To this complex framework must be added the action of the supervisory authorities as regards the financial system. Ensuring banks' solvency requires a substantial increase in their capital base, obtained through massive recapitalization operations aimed at fulfilling the new and more stringent capital requirements and creating the buffers necessary to guarantee 'business as usual' even in adverse economic conditions. The raising of new capital has not always been successful, given that weak profitability does not repay investors for the higher level of risk that now characterizes the banking sector, and market sentiment (measured through the price-to-book value) remains neutral, or even negative, as regards the banking system (CGFS, 2018).

The long decade of crisis has also been characterized by major structural changes: the increasingly pervasive diffusion of technology (internet and mobile) in daily life has radically changed user behavior with regard to banking services. Banking tools and applications not requiring the physical presence of a customer in a branch have increased exponentially, rendering a traditional network of brick-and-mortar branches superfluous. The problem from the economic point of view for the bank is therefore twofold: on the one hand, the costs necessary to guarantee speed and security for transactions carried out online increase with the progress of technology and its related, ever more sophisticated risks; on the other hand, the brick-and-mortar branch network continues to generate costs (buildings, equipment and maintenance, human resources, etc.) that are not easily compressible.

1.5 Cost Efficiency and Credit Quality: Merging Soft and Hard Information

As we have seen above, the troubled periods experienced by the banking system over the last decade have been determined by a number of closely interrelated factors. Macroeconomic aspects have had inevitable repercussions on the strictly managerial sphere, inducing banks to fully overhaul the strategies adopted up until then. Historically, there have been many banking crises, but they were almost always linked to poor management or episodes of misconduct by the directors; only in some cases (Barth et al., 2004; Logan, 2001) can a 'systemic' crisis be blamed, but which in any case was limited to a specific category of banks (US Saving and Loans, British small banks) and limited to one (albeit nationwide) area.

Analysts' predictions regarding the banking sector have always been positive, and rightly so; despite the fact that in years of economic difficulty even banks were affected by changed conditions, their performance was always positive. With the development of international markets and the increasing financialization of the economy, banking sector profitability has been largely assured by higher volumes of transactions, by the increasing sophistication of transactions, justifying high brokerage commissions, and by the increasing number of people who used banking services. Although it has never reached the record levels of certain sectors (e.g. the IT sector at the end of the last century and the dot.com phenomenon; Howcroft, 2001; Preissl et al., 2004), banking has been still considered profitable, and no one doubted the persistence of these profits over time. For these very reasons, listed bank shares have been always included in investors' value portfolios. In essence, bankers considered profits as 'guaranteed'; management objectives were established solely in terms of activity volumes and deriving revenues, allowing management costs to 'accompany' growth, without worrying too much about their increase.

The only possible element of concern was a growing level of competitiveness which, as of the 1980s, began to emerge in the banking sector, thanks to excellent assured returns. Moreover, it was the supervisory authorities themselves that encouraged an increasing level of competitiveness: the removal of structural regulatory constraints, together with the relaxation of most entrance restrictions, allowed the entry of new general or specialized operators into the financial intermediation market. The aim was to minimize costs for end users; from the regulator's point of view, the development of more competition leads to a reduction in prices charged (i.e. banks' revenues), and so greater attention to costs incurred. In fact, apart from urban areas where accentuated competitiveness resulted in the opening of numerous branches, the persistence of certain obstacles, such as sociodemographic characteristics and the productive system in certain areas, as well as the physical distance characterizing branches in rural areas in an era when banking could only be carried out at the branch, allowed banks to maintain a solid customer relationship base, thus ensuring competitive advantages.

The real turning point was the advent of computerized banking services, in that technological innovation rendered a customer's physical presence at the branch superfluous and drastically reduced the time required for transactions, while also limiting errors. Despite the significant investment necessary to implement new IT structures and guarantee absolute security to transactions, clients demanded reductions in charges for the various services; faster transactions and a lack of human intervention increased their perception of lower transaction costs. Banks were thus obliged to review their structural strategies and to rethink their activity.

The unfolding of the financial crisis coincided with mass digitization and a growing level of sophistication and security in online banking services; branches witnessed drastically reduced volumes of transactions and became useless and often expensive 'monuments' of the past. Undoubtedly, brick-and-mortar branches maintain their intrinsic economic value in that it is difficult to obtain soft information at a distance or through completely automated operations, and it is even more complex to categorize them univocally. Nevertheless, the high costs necessary to sustain a modus operandi of this type, together with higher costs deriving from the long period of crisis (losses on credit, costs deriving from more stringent regulation, etc.), induced banks to automate the collection of data and other information as much as possible, transforming it into 'hard' information; high levels of staff are maintained only in transactions involving significant amounts and high added value (wealth management, corporate finance transactions, etc.).

Lending is the operating segment most affected by this change, largely due to the Basel II regulations that obliged credit institutions to assign a rating to each borrower on the basis of objective and documented factors. Attribution to a certain class of risk implies a different capital requirement for the bank, which reaches a maximum in the event of absence or non-allocation of this rating (BCBS, 2006). The emphasis placed on the rating as a decisive element in the evaluation of a client's reliability, and consequently on the interest rate applied to the loan, certainly has the advantage of making the evaluation process objective, but does not permit full appreciation of soft information that cannot be processed by evaluation metrics. Despite the significant implementation costs of an internal rating-based model (legislation on the characteristics the model must possess is very stringent; BCBS, 2006, 2017), and the necessary validation by the supervisory authorities for its effective activation and its constant maintenance, many banks, especially larger ones, have decided to introduce this procedure as a key element in the decisional process when granting loans to their customers. The adoption of the new Basel II rules (June 2004, although the first version dates back to 1999) and the emergence of the first signs of the crisis (starting from 2007) appear too close in time to allow an objective assessment of the weight that the internal models of valuation may have had in credit quality deterioration, but it is clear that exclusive reliance on automated instruments may not capture some, often very significant, elements of evaluation; however, it is also true that the imposition of objective processes drastically reduces subjectivity in loan-granting decisions that, in some cases, caused serious difficulties for the bank, leading to real problems of solvency. The development of the financial crisis, which then also involved the 'real' sector pervasively, does not permit a clear separation of the causes of credit deterioration so heavily suffered in bank credit quality. Even the most virtuous banks, often in closer contact with the area in which their customers operate, nevertheless experienced high levels of NPLs. On these aspects, academic debate and the supervisory bodies' research have provided ample, although not always concordant, contributions, to which reference is made (Bonaccorsi di Patti and Gobbi, 2001; Duke, 2010; Brainard, 2015; Catturani and Stefani, 2016).

Examination of banks' income statement data would seem to reveal two major consequences: the first, of a cyclical nature, consists of NPLs, now in significant attenuation for almost all credit institutions after drastic balance sheet cleaning operations; the second, of a structural nature, is represented by a rigid (increasing) costs structure, against stable or decreasing revenues. In a context of reduced economic growth, with numerous uncertainties at the geopolitical level and low interest rates forecast for a further period, cost-cutting will represent the real challenge for the banking system in the coming years, especially in Europe. If this is clear from supervisory authorities' forecasts, and to international bodies (ECB, BIS and IMF), bankers believe it is decidedly less worrying: the reduction of operational inefficiencies is in fact only fifth on a list of bankers' concerns, which are focused more on macroeconomic and/or competitive aspects (Fig. 1.4).

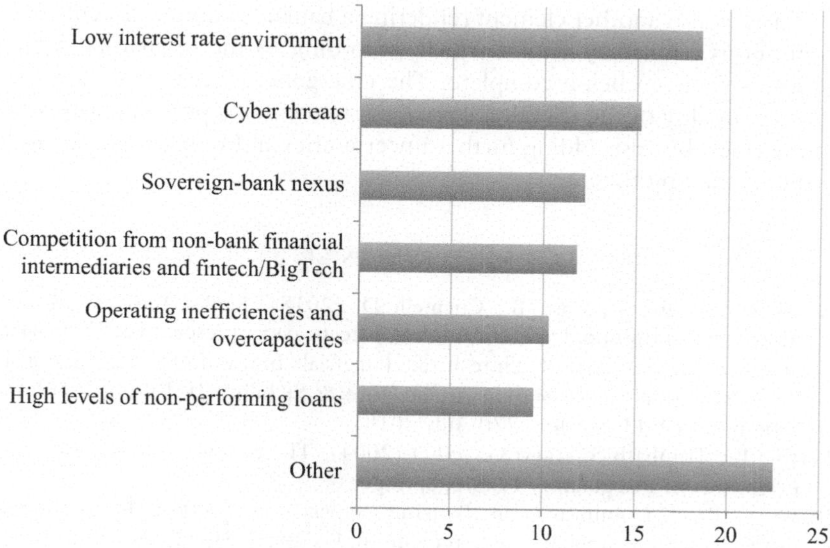

Fig. 1.4 Main challenges within the banking sector. Source: Adapted from ECB (2018). Percentages; challenges ranked by allocating a total of 100 points across the different risks

1.6 Conclusions

The great financial crisis generated significant changes in banking activity. The long protraction of periods of weak, when not negative, profitability has rendered many credit institutions more fragile; regulatory measures insisting on the further strengthening of own funds have pushed bankers to the continuous, and not easy, search for new capital; competition has become increasingly fierce, partly as a result of the entry into the market of new non-bank operators; macroeconomic uncertainties make the identification of business development strategies even more complicated.

In this complex framework, banks face important management challenges: deep 'cleansing' of their balance sheets, often still affected by large volumes of non-performing or unlikely-to-pay loans; determined improvement in the efficiency of organizational structures, especially in the area of transactional banking; the urgent definition of operational strategies within the fintech area. Otherwise they face a rapid reduction in profit margins (particularly in the area of payment services) and progressive marginalization on the market.

There is also another element rendering a banker's choices difficult: the continuous regulatory output which, according to the regulators themselves, is far from being complete. The emergence of new risks and the relative fragility of the traditional credit system entail a permanent review of the rules, but risk adding further uncertainties and weighing on banks' profits for a long time.

References

Ayadi R., Bongini P., Casu B., Cucinelli D. (2018), Banks' Business Model Migrations in Europe: Determinants and Effects, paper presented at "Financial Stability Implications of Fintech & Financial Innovation", International Workshop on Financial System Architecture & Stability (IWFSAS), London, September 10–11 (version: 27th July 2018).

Barth J.R., Trimbath S., Yago G. (eds.) (2004), The Savings and Loan Crisis: Lessons from a Regulatory Failure, Springer.

BCBS – Basel Committee on Banking Supervision (2006), International Convergence of Capital Measurement and Capital Standards. A Revised Framework. Comprehensive Version, June.

BCBS – Basel Committee on Banking Supervision (2017), Basel III: Finalising post-crisis reforms, December.

BIS – Bank for International Settlements (2018), Annual Economic Report.

Bonaccorsi di Patti, E., Gobbi, G. (2001), The changing structure of local credit markets: Are small business special?, Journal of Banking and Finance, 25: 2209–2237.

Brainard L. (2015), Community banks, small business credit, and online lending, Speech at the Community Banking in the 21st Century, The Third Annual Community Banking Research and Policy Conference, cosponsored by the Federal Reserve System and Conference of State Bank Supervisors, Federal Reserve Bank of St. Louis, St. Louis, Missouri, 30 September.

Catturani I., Stefani M.L. (2016), Italian Credit Cooperative Banks, in Karafolas S. (eds.), Credit Cooperative Institutions in European Countries. Contribution to Economics, Springer Cham.

CGFS – Committee on the Global Financial System (2018), Structural changes in banking after the crisis, CGFS Papers No. 60, January.

Chishti S., Barberis J. (eds.) (2016), The FinTech Book. The Financial Technology Handbook for Investors, Entrepreneurs and Visionaries, Wiley.

Claessens S., Frost J., Turner G., Zhu F. (2018), Fintech credit markets around the world: size, drivers and policy issues, BIS Quarterly Review, September.

Constancio V. (2016), Challenges for the European banking industry, conference "European Banking Industry: what's next?", University of Navarra, 7 July.

Constancio V. (2017), Resolving Europe's NPL burden: challenges and benefits, Keynote speech at an event entitled "Tackling Europe's non-performing loans crisis: restructuring debt, reviving growth" organised by Bruegel, Brussels, 3 February.

Demirgüç-Kunt A., Klapper L., Singer D., Ansar S., Hess J. (2018), The Global Findex Database 2017: Measuring Financial Inclusion and the Fintech Revolution, World Bank Group.

Dermine J. (2016), Digital banking and market disruption: a sense of *déja vu*?, Banque de France, Financial Stability Review, no. 20, April.

Detken C., Peltonen T. (eds.) (2017), A new database for financial crises in European countries, European Systemic Risk Board, Occasional Paper Series, No. 13, July.

Duke E.A. (2010), Small business lending, Testimony of Ms Elizabeth A Duke, Member of the Board of Governors of the Federal Reserve System, before the Committee on Financial Services and Committee on Small Business, US House of Representatives, Washington DC, 26 February.

EBA – European Banking Authority (2017), Risk Assessment of the European Banking System, November.

ECB – European Central Bank (2017), Report on financial structures, October.

ECB – European Central Bank (2018), Summary of Banking Industry Dialogue on 7 November 2018 in Frankfurt am Main, 27 November.

ECB Banking Supervision (2018), SSM thematic review on profitability and business model. Report on the outcome of the assessment, September.

ESRB – European Systemic Risk Board (2014), Is Europe Overbanked?, Reports of the Advisory Scientific Committee.

ESRB – European Systemic Risk Board (2017), A new database for financial crises in European countries, Occasional Paper Series, No 13/July.

FSB – Financial Stability Board (2017), Financial Stability Implications from FinTech, 27th June.

FSI – Financial Stability Institute (2018), The identification and measurement of non-performing assets: a cross-country comparison, FSI Insights on policy implementation, Bank of International Settlements, No. 7, April.

Howcroft D. (2001), After the goldrush: deconstructing the myths of the dot. com market, Journal of Information Technology, volume 16, Issue 4, pp. 195–204.

IMF – International Monetary Fund (2017), Global Financial Stability Report: Getting the Policy Mix Right, April.

IMF – International Monetary Fund (2018), Global Financial Stability Report: A Decade after the Global Financial Crisis: Are We Safer?, October.

Jobst A., Weber A. (2016), Profitability and Balance Sheet Repair of Italian Banks, IMF Working Paper, WP/16/175.

Logan A. (2001), The United Kingdom's small banks' crisis of the early 1990s: what were the leading indicators of failure?, Bank of England Working Paper 139.
McKinsey (2017), Retail Banking Insights, April.
Panetta F. (2018), Fintech and banking: today and tomorrow, Harvard Law School Bicentennial, Annual Reunion of the Harvard Law School Association of Europe, 12 May.
Preissl B., Bouwman H., Steinfield C. (2004), E-Life after the Dot Com Bust, Springer.
Reinhart C.M., Rogoff K.S. (2009), This Time is Different. Eight Centuries of Financial Folly, Princeton University Press.
Roengpitya R., Tarashev N.A., Tsatsaronis K., Villegas A. (2017), Bank Business Models: Popularity and Performance, BIS Working Paper No. 682, December.
World Economic Forum (2017), Beyond Fintech: A Pragmatic Assessment of Disruptive Potential In Financial Services, August.

CHAPTER 2

Bank Profitability: Measures and Determinants

Abstract This chapter deals with the choice of effective bank profitability measures, examining the strengths and weaknesses of the most widespread indices adopted in the literature and among practitioners. In particular, the main profitability and risk-adjusted return metrics are analyzed, comparing the different methodologies with which they can be calculated. In addition, a critical view of the ways in which they can be used in quantitative analysis is provided. Finally, the chapter contains an extensive review of the literature on the subject of determinants of bank profitability.

Keywords Profitability measures • Risk-adjusted profits • Efficiency • Troubled loans • Determinants of profits

2.1 Introduction

The bottom line has always been one of the main concerns of a for-profit company. The generation of a positive economic result is a precondition for the survival of a firm, permitting the accumulation of resources and the remuneration of the company's stakeholders. While the term 'profit' is in general easily defined, in the light of its strong link with the regulations governing business balance sheets, it is perhaps more appropriate here to talk about the 'profitability' of a company. Several aspects

M. Borroni, S. Rossi, *Banking in Europe*, Palgrave Macmillan Studies in Banking and Financial Institutions,
https://doi.org/10.1007/978-3-030-15013-6_2

contribute to the problematic issue of defining and measuring profitability, as used in financial language; this is even more so with reference to a complex entity such as a bank.

Profitability can be defined as the ability to produce a positive balance between the revenues and costs of an economic entity, be this a whole enterprise or a part of it, through the use of financial and non-financial resources. This means, first of all, that the measurement of bank profitability normally provides for a calculation in which the numerator contains items extracted from the income statement, while the denominator comprises items typically linked to assets or liabilities included in the balance sheet. The specific choice of the items that will be included in the calculation determines the wide range of indices available for analysis. The difference between costs and revenues, for example, can refer to the entire income statement or to specific areas of interest (for example, loans, trading activities). The result obtained (profits or other margins deriving from reclassifications in the financial statement) is therefore considered in relation to many figures extracted from the bank's balance sheet, such as total assets, equity or risk-weighted assets. Furthermore, from a temporal point of view, profitability can be measured at a set point or set points (for example, considering the quarterly, half-yearly or annual results), or calculated as an average of values over longer time horizons. To all of this we can, of course, add other indicators that refer to market data for companies listed on stock exchanges, expanding the term 'profitability' from the financial statement aspect to include changes in the value of securities held by shareholders (and other holders of the bank's financial liabilities). In reality, each analyst (and each researcher) adopts a set of indicators that s/he considers the most informative and reliable, and it is not possible to delineate a set of indexes judged incontrovertible in describing bank profitability. However, there are some properties, listed below, that appear particularly desirable when choosing a profitability metric.

The first characteristic should be consistency with the purpose for which the index was constructed. In particular, the quantities taken into consideration should effectively represent the analyst's area of interest; appropriate reclassifications in financial statements should make it possible to isolate those items that refer to similar activities performed by the bank, allowing a correct measurement of performance. Similarly, the measure should be consistent with the interests of the subject who intends to carry out an analysis of the bank's performance (for example, shareholders, whose earnings are not linked solely to the generation of profits during a financial year). Note that following this criterion can sometimes lead to a partial vision of bank profitability. For example, when focusing only on borrowing and lending activities, one could lose track of the virtues deriving from an income diversification policy. This aspect must be carefully assessed and clearly communicated when data analyses are performed, at the cost of providing biased information or misleading policy implications.

A second and fundamental characteristic should be data reliability: this involves some important considerations on the subject of data quality. Anyone who has carried out research using data extracted from bank balance sheets has experienced numerous problems in this regard: missing data, abnormal values, severe outliers, etc. The common saying 'garbage in, garbage out' explains in a crude but effective way the outcome of low data reliability: if analyses are based on corrupt or incomplete data, the result can only be a set of strongly biased results.

This aspect of data is strongly linked to a third virtuous element that should always be sought: data consistency. The existence of multiple methodologies for calculating the financial statement indices and the evolution over time of accounting principles and supervisory regulations make comparison between banks from different geographical contexts (a typical example is any comparison of European and U.S. banks) or the reconstruction of adequate historical series of data extremely complex. The risk, in these cases, is of obtaining highly distorted estimates due to the accounting method for some items, rewarding or penalizing unfairly the banks under investigation. The existence of different principles from country to country (even within apparently homogeneous areas such as the Banking Union) and the flexibility accorded to banks in the computation of some items on their own balance sheets undermine the comparability of results and represent issues that are difficult to overcome. To this is added the wide range of off-balance sheet values that are present in banking activity and which weaken any ability to measure the real worth of the financial amounts on which the bank bases its business. It is clear that the creation and use of bank profitability metrics requires a common framework of accounting rules and homogeneous practices in the calculation of the indices; in this field, the road ahead is still very long.

Alongside the three properties mentioned above, we would like to draw attention to two further elements that make it possible to increase the effectiveness of profitability measures in explaining the performance of a bank: these are elements that could be defined as 'enhancers' of the above properties.

The first element is transparency, meaning the possibility of clearly identifying and breaking down the determinants of profitability. This aspect is particularly important for 'aggregate' performance measures, that is, those that consider the bank's net profits; in this case, the overall result is the sum of many different values, and therefore the possibility of identifying and measuring the individual components of the calculation provides valuable indications. It is evident that this property is fundamental for managerial implications deriving from the analysis of profitability sources, as it permits the identification of sources of revenue and costs for the bank. An increase in profits can be achieved both by increasing the sources of revenue and by acting on the cost side; however, both strategies have some drawbacks. The former could be achieved by increasing the degree of risk of the investments (or activities) carried out, or by activating areas of business previously absent from the bank's offer; however, this would translate into higher costs for the acquisition of skilled enough personnel to conduct new business lines or a general increase in business risk. The second strategy is often used to cope with crisis phenomena: cost-cutting is in fact a common reaction from a managerial point of view in the face of a reduction in revenues. However, the depletion of resources (human and/or technological) available to the bank risks reducing the quality of services offered to customers or the effectiveness of organizational, managerial and control safeguards within the company, leading to even more threats, putting the very survival of the bank at risk. Being able to isolate and analyze individually the items that produce the bank profitability metric makes the process of data interpretation much more effective.

The second element comprises the replicability of the result; the greater the information content of a given profitability datum, the greater the persistence of profits. This aspect is of fundamental importance in the analysis of bank profitability, being linked to the bank's ability to increase its equity over time, attract new capital and reduce its overall risk. The volatility of a company's financial results makes the estimation of its value more complex (e.g. models used for estimating the fair value of the shares, whose forecasting capacity of profit flows is fundamental for determining the timespan of securities' evaluation) and, more generally, constitutes an element of risk for stakeholders. It is not by chance that the volatility of financial results is used to build numerous measures of risk-adjusted return, often far more informative than simple profitability values.

From the above it is clear how complex it is to have effective measures of profitability; each usable metric has strengths and weaknesses that must be taken into account when interpreting the financial performance of a bank. Except for surveys that aim to study specific areas of a bank's balance sheet, it would therefore be preferable to use a set of different profitability measures in order to conduct appropriate cross-checks between results, and robustness checks. This strategy also permits accounting for the distinctive features of a bank's balance sheet structure, which often makes use of specific asset and liability construction choices. From this point of view, a certain degree of leverage, a focus on traditional banking activity rather than trading or fee-based activities, or operating through off-balance sheet instruments, can have a significant impact on the dynamics of the different profitability measures, as we will see later.

Likewise, the need to extend the traditional cross-sectional view of the bank's financial performance toward panel analysis is also clear. This decision involves some technical complexities, but has an undeniable advantage in terms of analysis robustness and economic significance of the results. The use of panel data makes it possible to use econometric estimation models that are more effective in describing the relationships between the variables. In the same way, with datasets covering adequate timespans, it is possible to explore the effects of changes occurring in the relationships between the variables themselves over time, rendering the analysis dynamic rather than static. However, there are numerous obstacles to the construction of effective databases for analysis; indeed, the longer the historical series, the more the missing data, mergers and acquisitions (M&As) and variations in accounting standards. It is no coincidence that in the literature, there are few cases of research using highly detailed balance sheet items and extending for periods of over 15–20 years.

In the light of these observations, it would be reasonable to imagine that the literature on bank profitability is considerable, and that the range of indicators used to measure the financial performance of banks is equally wide. In reality, the first statement is certainly true; the second can be considered, as a rule, false. Countless studies have explored the theme of bank profitability, generally trying to investigate the factors that tend to explain its trend. The bank profitability measures used by these research works, on the contrary, are generally traceable to three main indices. In most cases, the key variable is the return on equity (ROE), to which the return on assets (ROA) and the net interest margin (NIM) may be added (or sometimes replace it). These measures owe their popularity to numerous factors: of these, their ease of access and calculation, and the simplicity with which it is possible to interpret their values, stand out. The requirement for banks to provide balance sheets subject to numerous controls makes these indicators appealing and widely adopted among researchers, analysts and practitioners; they are also the only method of investigation for banks unlisted on stock exchanges, for which, therefore, no market data exist.

Over time, volatility measures for these indicators (generally in the form of standard deviation) and risk-return variables have also been established; examples of these latter ratios are the RAROA and RAROE, respectively, obtained by dividing the ROA and ROE by their volatility over time. These are interesting extensions to bank profitability analysis, since, as stated previously, persistence is a fundamental element for the evaluation of the overall performance achieved by a company.

Given that profitability and its variability over time influence (or put at risk) the resilience of the bank, we might ideally also add to this list metrics created primarily with the aim of measuring the bank's ability to bear risk, as, for example, the Z-Score. Below all these profitability measures are analyzed in detail, in an attempt to highlight their reporting content, areas of use and critical aspects.

2.2 Profitability Measures: ROE, ROA and NIM

2.2.1 ROE

Of the various bank profitability measures, ROE (return on equity) is without a doubt the most well-known metric used in the scientific and professional world. It is an indicator that is easy to construct and use, its financial significance is extremely simple to understand and it is available for all companies, even those not listed on regulated markets. It is therefore not surprising that in the bank profitability literature, ROE has been used as a dependent variable in most quantitative studies. At the same time, this index is the classic unit of measurement used by analysts to monitor a company's ability to make itself profitable over time; managers usually communicate the ROE as a measure of realized or prospective performance, knowing that the market easily understands the meaning of this financial metric.

However, a habitual use of a certain parameter or financial indicator involves risks, one of which is a tendency toward uniformity, routine, uncritical choice. Indeed, alignment with mainstream thought leads to a reinforcing of the use of variables that are known in the literature, neglecting other potentially better ones. This behavior is true both of the research world and among practitioners; as previously stated, managers tend to communicate their expectations to the market, using the more commonly used variables in order to facilitate understanding of their results. The choice of innovative variables could therefore be perceived as a form of deviation from the consolidated best practice and recognized as such by the financial world, generating resistance from the end users of the data. However, innovation often signals progress, an attempt to improve the status quo of a certain field of study, and this may also be true in the field of measuring the performance of a bank. The ROE, although undoubtedly having its qualities, is far from being a faultless indicator of bank profitability (ECB, 2018).

ROE is generally calculated as the ratio between net income and owners' equity at the end of a certain period of observation. The latter usually tends to coincide with the end of the calendar year, unless the drawing up of financial statements requires different choices. The importance that this indicator has acquired over time derives from the significance that can be attributed to it: the ROE expresses the percentage of remuneration obtained by shareholders through net profits recorded in the company's income statement. This is a fundamental information for the shareholders in that they can compare this result with the profitability offered by other instruments or the stock market as a whole, verifying whether the risk-return profile of their investment meets their expectations. This aspect is particularly useful when determining whether the company is creating or destroying value, for example, by comparing its ability to generate a level of profitability sufficient to cover its weighted average cost of capital or, more simply, its expected cost of equity. Other measures of evaluation of a company and its management (e.g. EVA and similar models), which moreover often underlie top management incentive policies and remuneration, depend on these comparisons. In addition, the ROE is included in the valuation models of equity securities, such as the dividend discount model, as a growth promoter: the latter is calculated by multiplying the ROE by the rate of self-financing of a company. There is therefore no doubt that the reputation of ROE rests on solid bases.

However, as stated previously, this parameter has numerous weak points which must be taken into due consideration. The first is a feature common to almost all financial indices and derives from the possibility of there being different ways of calculating a certain parameter. For example, in the case of ROE, profits can be considered gross or net of some specific items; a classic example of this is the treatment of the tax component. If one wants to compare companies belonging to different economic contexts, and therefore subject to different income tax rules, it would be more appropriate to use an ROE gross of these cost components; it is also true that the existence of a certain tax treatment could have justified the start of a business activity in a certain country, potentially rendering the previous methodological choice unsound. The selection of the most appropriate parameter must therefore be assessed carefully on the basis of the specific characteristics of the analysis being carried out and the specificities of the sample examined.

Likewise, the choice of denominator may include only a few items or the whole of shareholders' equity; however, unless there are justifications for making specific exclusions, the second choice usually appears preferable. Again with reference to the denominator, but this time considering the time profile at which the index is calculated, the ROE can be based on the owners' equity recorded at the close of the financial statements or on the average of this balance sheet aggregate at the beginning and end of the period considered. In the latter case, it would be more appropriate to talk about return on average equity (ROAE), in order to underline the difference in calculation compared to the traditional version of the index. Note, however, that it is quite common to find both versions under the name ROE. From a financial and interpretative point of view, the index calculated on the average of the owners' capital appears more correct; in fact, if a tangible change in the shareholders' equity occurred during the year, a denominator formed only from the stock at the end of the period risks providing biased results. For example, a bank that at the beginning of the year had owners' equity of 100, and that saw this balance sheet item increase to 200 at the end of the year, if it had a net income of 12, would have an ROE of 6% and an ROAE of 8%. Likewise, if the same bank at the beginning of the year possessed owners' equity of 200 and if this item was reduced to 100 at the end of the year, if it recorded the same net income of 12, it would have an ROE of 12% and an ROAE of 8%. Hence, like all measures calculated as the average of observations, the ROAE has a smoothing effect on the dynamics of a company's profitability: in particular, it underestimates (overestimates) profitability in the event of a reduction (increase) in the equity during the year. However, this feature has a financial significance: using the average of owners' equity enables one to account for the fact that the production of net profits occurred during the year, thanks to a certain average capital endowment. A calculation made using single-point data would crystallize the bank's financial situation at a certain date, losing sight of the dynamic aspects of the phenomenon examined. Obviously, this assumption too presents potential defects. The average of the balances at the beginning and at the end of the year implies that it is assumed that the change observed in shareholders' equity occurred proportionally throughout the year; if instead it happened near the beginning or the end, the calculation would provide biased results.

There is another highly critical aspect of the ROE, which derives from the very information used to construct the indicator: the company's operational sensitivity to financial leverage. This is a delicate problem in the light of the effects that the correlation between the two variables can produce on interpretations of the ROE data provided by a company. Indeed, all else being equal, a company with less owners' equity will have a higher ROE. Since this index is so widespread and appreciated, this could push managers to choose more leveraged financial structures in order to increase the perception of profitability of their companies. This aspect is well known in the financial and banking field in particular; the international financial crisis that began in 2007 clearly highlighted both the extreme level of leverage with which some financial intermediaries operated, and the risks that this strategy involves. Increased leverage weakens the financial structure of a bank, making it more vulnerable and less resilient to losses. It could be argued that the increase in ROE as leverage increases represents compensation (through greater profitability) for the greater risks incurred by shareholders; however, in the absence of an adequate perception of this growing risk, the increase in ROE would be seen as the result of better business management. It is also no coincidence that prudential regulation has imposed precise and more stringent limits on leverage in the banking sector due to episodes of instability that affected many banks during the crisis. Some of the ROE reduction observed after 2007 in European banks (see Chap. 3) must therefore also be linked to the increase in the stock of shareholders' equity and not just to a contraction of net profits: the greater capital endowment today characterizing the banking system should, however, exclude a return to the levels of ROE observed before the financial crisis that began in 2007.

2.2.2 ROA

ROA (return on assets) is the second most used performance measure (after ROE) in the banking sector; in the literature, it is extremely common to find both measures as dependent variables in econometric estimations or in financial analysts' reports. In particular, ROA is used together with ROE to verify differences in the behavior of covariates when the dependent variable varies, or as an alternative to ROE in empirical model robustness checks.

In the financial world, ROA is widely used, thanks to the ease with which it is possible to interpret its results: it permits measurement of the return generated by a company's assets. This is because the indicator is constructed by relating the bank's net income to its total assets. As in the previous case, some indexes are constructed by putting the average of total assets at the beginning and at the end of the observation period in the denominator, rather than the final value obtained from the balance sheet; in these cases, we speak of ROAA, or return on average assets.

Summarizing the differences between these performance indicators, it can be affirmed that while ROE focuses on the return generated for shareholders, ROA expresses the result obtained from the use of the company's assets, regardless of the way in which they were financed. From this point of view, the use of ROA is particularly interesting, since it shifts attention on the one hand onto the managerial choices behind the composition of the assets, and on the other onto the profitability of the latter. This aspect is linked to some key strategic choices for a bank, such as the identification of its business model and risk appetite.

Indeed, two main aggregates tend to prevail in the assets of a bank: the banking book and the trading book. The so-called "commercial banks" are usually characterized by a significant presence of loans in their total assets: their prevailing activity is the traditional role of the banking system, that is, borrowing and lending money. The prevalence of the banking book means these banks are particularly sensitive to deterioration of the creditworthiness of their clients and market interest rate trends. On the contrary, the so-called "investment banks" are less exposed in terms of loans granted to customers; for them, the trading book and financial investment in general are more important. These banks are therefore more vulnerable to market instability and the decline in listings and M&A transactions.

Banking books and trading books present different profitability profiles over time, and therefore banks typically expand or reduce these asset areas for strategic purposes, while maintaining the distinctive characteristics of their business model. From this point of view, the two events of, firstly, the severe international crisis, and then the sovereign income crisis, have shown how all the areas in which a bank employs its assets can generate severe problems; an ability to adapt to these stimuli renders revenue structure more flexible and increases a bank's resilience.

The profitability generated by banking books and trading books allows for an increase in ROA (and also in ROE), but it is obviously linked to the risk of the underlying assets. This aspect must be examined carefully; the presence (ceteris paribus) of higher returns without an increase in risk must, in fact, be seen as an anomaly destined to be neutralized over time. Prudential regulation requires that banks work carefully on these aspects, where it requires that the risk appetite framework identifies precise qualitative and quantitative parameters for the establishment of risk appetite, risk tolerance and risk capacity. The ROA data should therefore be examined in light of these preliminary analyses, in order to verify the risk-return profile of the bank's business and not just its mere profitability. This issue is linked to a more general finding: a change in the profitability of a certain business area or a switch between different areas always involves a cost in terms of risk or new skills required by the bank. The increase in profitability must therefore be examined over time (in terms of expected persistence) and in terms of a risk-return analysis.

Net of these observations, there is no doubt that ROA lends itself to providing indications regarding bank profitability; however, some additional strengths and weaknesses of this parameter should be examined. Among the strengths, apart from the ease of reading and understanding mentioned above, return on assets normally has a low volatility over time; this is also true in cross-sectional comparison of bank samples, where the dispersion of ROA data is often limited. This aspect is immediately evident where comparison is made between ROE and ROA; not being influenced by leverage, the ROA has much more stable and homogeneous values in sample analyses or time series, facilitating the process of comparison and analysis. At the same time, this reduced variability makes it difficult to make effective distinctions between subjects: often, in fact, the differences between banks' ROAs are so limited that they do not permit clear distinctions between those characterized by higher profitability levels.

One of the main limitations of ROA is linked to an accounting aspect of this financial parameter: if a bank has significant amounts of off-balance-sheet activities, the ROA tends to provide biased results, that is, to lose real financial significance. Unfortunately, as stated earlier, accounting practices have traveled a long way in terms of international convergence over the last few decades, but significant areas of uncertainty still remain on the computability and measurement of numerous items that are part of banking business. In this regard, it could even be said that market awareness of the existence of large shares of off-balance-sheet assets in banks' balance sheets has led to a progressive loss of confidence in the ROA.

2.2.3 NIM

The NIM (net interest margin) represents the third and final "classical" measure by which bank profitability is assessed: it represents the return obtained through traditional intermediation activity, that is, borrowing and lending money. More specifically, the indicator is usually constructed by dividing net interest income by interest-earning assets; net interest income is, in turn, calculated as the difference between interest income (derived from the bank-lending activity) and interest expenses (paid to those who lend to the bank, such as account holders). For this index too, there is a formulation (which is also the most frequent in the literature) which provides for the inclusion in the denominator of the average interest-earning assets as the average of the data collected at the beginning and at the end of the observation period.

Compared to the performance indicators mentioned above, NIM stands out for one fundamental reason: it takes into consideration only the revenues and costs incurred for the traditional activity of commercial banks, ignoring other forms of cost and revenue. This may appear to be an element of weakness in the index, due to the neglecting of many entries deriving from the bank's income statement; in fact, this focus on a few, but very significant budget items, allows us to examine the profitability of the bank's core business (at least for commercial banks) in greater depth. The NIM numerator, or net interest income, is one of the main items contributing to the net income of a bank (and therefore also influences the performance of other indices, such as ROE and ROA). A contraction in net interest income must be offset by the start-up or strengthening of business lines, by a reduction in operating costs or by leveraging non-recurring incomes; all these alternative strategies present different kinds of risks, which must be carefully examined.

Although it has always been a focus of attention among researchers and practitioners, NIM has grown in importance in the analysis of bank profitability following the great international financial crisis. After 2007, bank credit portfolios began to show signs of sharp deterioration; non-performing loans grew enormously, penalizing banks that operated with riskier customers and with a high share of loans over total assets. Small local banks focusing on traditional borrowing and lending activities have been strongly affected by these dynamics, but large international groups have also experienced critical issues. The monetary authorities' response to the rapid spread of the crisis in the economic system has involved various policies, but an extremely evident aspect has been the general lowering of short-term interest rates; in the more developed countries, this has been accompanied by a strong decrease in long-term rates, leading to a flattening of the yield curve. These two elements, of a micro- and macroeconomic nature (the formation of NPLs and the drastic lowering of rates of return), have an impact on NIM: they are able to influence (sometimes indirectly) both the denominator and the numerator of the index. The evolution of the net interest margin therefore has the role of showing how banks can adapt their asset and liabilities management following a change in the surrounding economic context, and hence the interest in this performance indicator in turbulent years such as those following 2007.

Alongside these undoubted qualities, NIM also naturally has some limitations. As previously stated, the first derives from its very nature; focusing only on net interest income, the index neglects other potential important business areas that the bank may decide to enter. Over the last few decades, the banking system has in fact become an access hub for multiple products and services that generate considerable revenue streams, according to a diversification model that regulatory and supervisory authorities have endorsed and, in some cases, promoted. Even if net interest income remains at the core of the profitability of commercial banks, the non-interest rate share often reaches values above 30–40% of operating revenues; NIM therefore risks providing a blurred and very rough photograph of a bank's ability to generate income.

A second critical aspect regards the inability of the net interest margin to disentangle the importance of interest income and interest costs in the calculation of net interest income. An increase in the NIM numerator could, in fact, derive from greater asset profitability or from cheaper funding sources; both situations have specific risk factors. An increase in interest incomes could, in fact, signal credit concession to riskier customers, willing to pay higher interest rates against their own risk of insolvency. Likewise, a reduction in the rate of interest on savings (e.g. through current accounts) could weaken customer loyalty, leading to cash outflows to the benefit of competitors or other uses by customers.

Finally, NIM does not take into account the degree of efficiency that characterizes the bank itself. Unlike the two indices described above, NIM does not contain any information on operating costs, being limited only to consideration of interest costs as an element of expenditure for the bank. This is a critical aspect in the light of the great importance that the issue of efficiency is assuming in the banking sector; in fact, margin compression renders a careful cost containment activity crucial in order to stabilize profitability results in the face of market turbulence.

2.3 Risk-Return Measures

The use of financial performance measures for the analysis of a bank's health status and future profitability prospects is certainly very common among financial market operators and supervisory authorities. As noted above, cross-sectional data analysis risks providing summary indications of poor reporting value. Indeed, a single performance does not throw any light on one fundamental aspect of bank profitability metrics: persistence. This property is extremely desirable in the context of a financial analysis of a company. It indicates management's ability to stabilize the company's profitability level. This involves limiting the impact of external factors (such as macroeconomic, competitive and regulatory factors) on the business, adopting appropriate strategic choices permitting generation of a constant flow of income. It is clear that all the bank's stakeholders benefit from this virtuous behavior: shareholders, who see earnings produced consistently; creditors, who perceive income stability as a sign of greater financial solidity; supervisory authorities, who see profit-generating capacity as a sign of individual intermediaries' stability.

Over the years, academics and practitioners have created a wide range of risk-adjusted return measures (the so-called RAPM, or risk-adjusted performance measures), with the aim of providing a clearer view of the link between positive financial performance and risks borne to achieve this result. This is an entirely natural evolution of the "raw" measures of performance examined above: from an interpretative point of view, a higher performance should be linked to greater risk-taking, according to well-known concepts rooted in financial theory. However, if a company succeeds in producing a risk-adjusted profitability higher than the sector it belongs to, thanks to specific factors including more prudent managerial choices, it can actually be considered preferable with respect to its competitors. So what are the risk-adjusted performance measures that can be used to measure bank profitability?

The literature on the topic has focused on some particularly significant and widespread indicators: RAROE, ROROA and Z-Score. This last indicator could appear an eccentric inclusion in this list, since it is traditionally associated with the issue of bank resilience and is therefore more a measure of financial soundness than a performance indicator. However, it is closely linked with the profitability and risk-adjusted return measures we are examining, and therefore presents elements of interest that we will detail below.

In general, the main risk-adjusted return measures are based on well-known risk metrics; of these, the most commonly used is the standard deviation. This statistical measure is widespread in modern finance, thanks to its simplicity of calculation and interpretation. It expresses the degree of volatility of a certain phenomenon, and therefore represents the classic degree of risk of an investment in the collective imagination. Standard deviation underlies two indices widely used in the literature: RAROE and RAROA. They are usually calculated as follows:

$$\text{RAROE} = \frac{\text{ROE}}{\sigma\text{ROE}}$$

$$\text{RAROA} = \frac{\text{ROA}}{\sigma\text{ROA}}$$

where σROE and σROA, respectively, identify the calculated standard deviation for ROE and ROA over the reference period, which requires some clarification. As always occurs when calculating a single-point figure starting from a numerical series, it is necessary to first define the period on which the analysis is to be carried out; this depends simultaneously on the availability of data and the time span of interest. On the one hand, it should be noted that, as a rule, banks listed on regulated markets disclose financial data frequently; this allows for good-quality quarterly data series. On the other hand, unlisted banks tend to release financial statements annually, reducing the amount of information available for calculating the volatility of returns. This aspect is particularly important where it is necessary to calculate the RAROE and RAROA on an annual basis; in this case, the calculation is made possible, thanks to the presence of quarterly data that allow estimation of profit volatility for each single year. In the case of annual data, it is necessary to proceed with the calculation of volatility over longer periods, losing much of the detail in the data. Although this aspect is crucial for research work on panel data, which is heavily penalized by the absence of quarterly data, it should be underlined that data transformation in a cross-sectional analysis, based on averages and standard deviation calculated over longer periods (for example, a cycle of 5–7 years), does appear to be consistent with a medium-term vision in the analysis of bank profitability.

From an interpretative point of view, the measures indicated above have the same characteristics as the metrics from which they derive, that is, ROE and ROA; they do, however, permit the penalizing of subjects with a high dispersion of financial results. An increase in the standard deviation reduces the RAROE and RAROA figures, compensating for any profitability peaks detected during the observation period. In this regard, a potential source of analytical weakness should be noted where a bank has particularly stable returns over time; in this case, volatility tends to zero, and the risk-adjusted measure tends to infinity, losing all numerical and interpretative significance. This is a rather frequent problem in empirical analysis, especially when working with quarterly data and with banks that pursue income-smoothing strategies; any low profitability could be offset by a low volatility of ROE and ROA, leading to particularly high levels of RAROE and RAROA. The result is a general indication; with composite metrics calculated using relationships between several financial values, the observation of single components is fundamental to understanding the dynamics of the compound index. When observing RAROE and RAROA data, it is therefore good practice to analyze in detail the profitability and profit volatility data that contributed to the calculation—a much clearer and more reliable view will be achieved.

There is a third measure used frequently in empirical work dealing with bank profitability: the Z-Score. As stated previously, this variable is mainly used in the analysis of bank resilience and, more specifically, bank stability. The formula by which the Z-Score is normally constructed is as follows:

$$\text{Z-Score} = \frac{(\text{car} + \text{ROA})}{\sigma\text{ROA}}$$

where car is equal to the bank's capital asset ratio (i.e. the ratio between equity and total assets) and σROA is equal to the standard deviation of the ROA. The index is clearly characterized by the numerator, which contains the solvency condition of the bank. Indeed, as a rule, insolvency occurs when the sum of car and ROA is null or negative; a high level of capitalization is therefore necessary to counteract negative ROA results. The volatility of ROA, seen in the index denominator, according to this view, penalizes companies that have shown an unstable pattern of financial results over time. Alongside these preliminary observations, examination of the previous equation highlights some peculiarities of the Z-Score. First of all, it is clear that the index is generally related to RAROA, from which it is mainly distinguished by the presence of the term that identifies the level of capitalization. This means the Z-Score has the qualities and defects of RAROA, as highlighted above.

A crucial aspect in the calculation and interpretation of the index is once again the time horizon over which the analysis is conducted; this is a very important issue, since an increase in the amount of information required for the calculation of the indicator forces numerous methodological choices. What surprises those approaching analysis of the Z-Score for the first time is the difficulty of finding a clear description of the way in which it was calculated in empirical works. In fact, there are numerous approaches that can be used to determine the Z-Score; they are distinguished by the way in which the three components comprising the index are treated from a statistical point of view. This is particularly important when calculating Z-Score values for a time series. Indeed, where only a cross-sectional photograph of a sample is to be provided, it is possible to calculate car, ROA and σROA as the means and standard deviations of the sample data over the entire observation period. If, on the other hand, one intends to make an estimation on panel data and thus underline the variation in time of the individual variables, it must be decided whether to implement a strategy based on moving windows or to use point data. This aspect has been directly analyzed in a work by Lepetit and Strobel (2013), which discusses the advantages and disadvantages of each method as used in the different strands of literature on the topic. The model proposed by the authors involves the calculation of ROA and sigma ROA, respectively, as mean and standard deviation of ROA over the entire reference period; the car is instead considered at the year examined. It is a solution that greatly reduces complexity of calculation and the problem of overlapping moving windows of numerical series; at the same time, the severe outliers deriving from excessively low or high standard deviations tend to be reduced due to the limited number of data on which they are calculated.

As stated at the outset, the set of financial metrics aiming to provide an effective measurement of bank profitability is very numerous; the examples referred to above are only a limited sample, albeit forming the basis of an extremely large number of empirical research works published in the main international journals. Table 2.1 provides a schematic representation of the indices present on some of the main databases from which it is possible to extract bank financials worldwide.

Some of the indices contained in Table 2.1 are used for comparing banks and are adopted in the RAF and ICAAP processes to provide a quantitative representation of the choices (and the subsequent results) of risk assumption and production of returns. In particular, we note the presence of numerous indicators that use risk-weighted assets as a scale variable; this is a choice of high reporting value, given the enormous importance that risk assumes in the rules concerning the adequacy of a bank's capital. The table also contains numerous indicators that provide a high degree of detail on the composition of revenue sources (an element that is linked to the bank's choice of business model); in particular, they highlight the indices that provide the degree of diversification of revenues, distinguishing between interest and non-interest income within operating revenue. Finally, it is interesting to note the progressive spread of indices constructed on tangible equity measures (based on the subtraction of intangible assets, including goodwill, from total equity); the financial crisis has, in fact, brought to the public's attention the need to make prudent assessments on the measurement and quality of equity, laying the foundations for new and more effective performance indicators.

To give a full picture, it is important to remember that other performance indicators, such as RAROC, RORAC, RARORAC and EVA, are found in the academic literature and in use among practitioners. Many of these indicators have a structural weakness: difficulty in obtaining the multiple, timely (and reliable) information on which they are built. Indeed, these are metrics that provide a high degree of detail in the estimates of many variables, and therefore lend themselves more to analysis carried out internally by the bank; even in this case, however, the quality of the data could be insufficient to carry out adequate evaluation (for example, due to inadequate internal reporting mechanisms and analytical accounting).

In the analysis conducted in Chap. 3, we will use several financial indicators, but in accordance with the content of the previous discussion,

Table 2.1 Profitability measures in two widely used databases

BvD Orbis BankFocus	
Net Interest Revenues/average assets	Return on risk-weighted assets (RoRWA) (operating profit/RWAs)
Other Operating Incomes/average assets	Recurring earning power (pre-impairment operating profit/average total assets)
Non Interest Expenses/average assets	Net interest margin (NIM)
Pre-Tax Operating Income/average assets	Interest income/average interest-earning assets
Non Operating items & taxes/average assets	Interest expense/average interest-bearing liabilities
Return on average assets (ROAA)	Net interest income/average risk-weighted assets (RWAs)
Return on average equity (ROAE)	Net fee and commission income/average risk-weighted assets (RWAs)
Dividend pay-out	Operating expense/average risk-weighted assets (RWAs)
Income net of Distributions/average equity	Net income/average risk-weighted assets (RWAs)
Non Operating items/net income	Net interest income/operating revenues
Cost-to-income ratio	Interest income on loans/average gross customer loans & advances
Recurring earning power	Interest expense on customer deposits/average customer deposits
Pre-impairment operating profit	Non-interest income/operating revenues
Net income	
	Cost to average asset ratio
Operating profit/average total equity	Dividends related to the period/net income
S&P SNL Market Intelligence	
Return on average assets (ROAA)	Pre-impairment operating profit/average assets
Return on average equity (ROAE)	Pre-impairment Operating Profit/Average risk-adjusted assets
Return on average ordinary equity	Pre-tax profit/average risk-adjusted assets
Return on average tangible ordinary equity	Net interest income/average risk-weighted assets
Return on average risk-weighted assets	Net fee income/average risk-weighted assets
Net interest margin	Operating expense/average risk-weighted assets
Net interest income/average assets	Cost-to-income
Net operating expense/average assets	Net interest income/operating revenue
Net fee income/average assets	Net fee & commissions/operating income
Operating expense/average assets	

focus our attention mainly on measures extracted from balance sheet data. This choice is also linked to the presence of numerous operators in the European banking market that are not listed on regulated markets. For these, the publication of their financials is the main source of transparency toward the outside world, and therefore analysis by external parties (researchers, financial analysts, etc.) must be carried out on these data.

2.4 Determinants of Bank Profitability: A Literature Review

After reviewing the advantages and disadvantages deriving from the use of each measure of profitability, we move on to an equally crucial aspect: in this paragraph, we analyze the factors that explain bank profitability according to causal links widely explored in the literature. Since this is a subject of enormous interest, it is not surprising to note that research works on bank profitability are particularly numerous; there are also many variables that have proved capable of explaining the dynamics of income produced by a bank. To try to simplify our analysis and make the contents more usable, it is important to firstly divide the main determinants of bank profitability into internal and external factors. Indeed, it is common practice in empirical research to link the income dynamics of a bank to factors linked, on the one hand to the organizational, competitive and financial choices made by top management, and on the other to context factors such as the business cycle trend, regulation and competitive pressure.

2.4.1 *Internal Determinants of Profitability*

The profitability of a company is usually determined by managerial choices regarding organization, production and strategy; these choices ensure reaction to external stimuli, anticipation of competitors' moves and improved efficiency of the company. Given this premise, it is legitimate to affirm that there is a direct link between managerial choices and the income profile of a bank; in other words, at least ideally, critical issues observable in the financials of a bank could be traced back to bad management in the first instance. This is due to the fact that the top management of a bank controls a wide range of elements affecting the profitability, the risk and therefore the stability of the company that they govern. We group these elements under the heading 'internal determinants of bank profitability'.

This is a large group of factors, extensively studied in empirical research that has tested over time their ability to affect the performance of banks, often finding conflicting results. This potentially destabilizing outcome, however, renders the issue of determinants of bank profitability always current and interesting, ensuring the theme does not crystallize into immutable axioms.

One of the most carefully explored factors among the determinants of bank profitability is the size of the bank. The size of a company is an extremely well-known and investigated topic in various fields of research, not just in the financial sphere. It is a factor that has multiple effects on the performance of a bank: on the one hand, it is linked to the possible creation of economies of scale (on this topic, Smirlock, 1985; Shehzad et al., 2013), while, on the other, large size can have specific connotations for some subjects (e.g. the so-called 'too big to fail' banks (SIFIs)), and condition their behavior and economic results. In the literature, size is a control variable present in almost all empirical work; its importance in discriminating small and large subjects is fundamental, above all, where the size range of the investigated samples is wide. For example, many European Union countries have microscopic banks (for example, small cooperative banks with very few brick-and-mortar branches) coexisting in the same market, with intermediaries operating on a global scale; in these cases, it is essential that the size of the subjects analyzed is considered carefully. However, the results of empirical estimation models concerning the role of size in influencing bank profitability provide contrasting results. The existence of economies of scale in banking business is not proven incontrovertibly; in general, the indications deriving from data analysis seem to suggest that the advantages linked to size decrease as the size increases (Goddard et al., 2004; Tregenna, 2009). This result should not be surprising: an increase in size can generate some beneficial scale effects, but at the same time it generates organizational diseconomies and various forms of inefficiency linked to the giant dimension itself. When the negative effects outweigh the positives, an increase in size becomes a negative factor for a bank's profitability. However, contrary cases may occur, in which small entities can exploit competitive advantages (for example, linked to geographical presence or highly specialized skills), generating high (and stable) levels of profitability. We can state that size may often represent a significant element in explaining a pattern of bank profitability; the sign of the link, however, is not certain a priori.

A second internal factor is the business model chosen by the bank (see Chap. 1). Indeed, there is no doubt that this element radically conditions the strategic positioning of the company and its return-risk profile (for a review of the literature on determinants of different business models, see Gambacorta and van Rixtel, 2013). Much research effort concentrated on this aspect in the period immediately following the great international financial crisis; this indirectly demonstrates the importance attributed to the choice of business model in explaining banks' income profile. The determination of a bank's orientation toward a certain business model can be carried out directly through specific dummies, where the strategic choice made by management is declared, or through variables that tend to capture specific and significant connotations of the bank's activity. Of these, two variables can be derived from, respectively, the balance sheet and the income statement of an intermediary: the share of loans out of total assets and the interest income (or non-interest income, as preferred).

The share of the credit portfolio out of a bank's total assets denotes its orientation toward the traditional activity of borrowing and lending money; in some cases, where the quality of the data is adequate for carrying out more refined analyses, it is possible to focus on specific types of loans, such as those aimed at retail clients. It is indeed reasonable to expect that wholesale and retail operations are characterized by different margin profiles for the bank; this consideration could also be extended to the liabilities side, in order to isolate the bank's ability to raise money from the retail public. The great financial crisis has shown how an orientation toward lending activity presents a contribution to bank profitability dependent on the characteristics of the economic cycle. During the years of dizzying growth in subprime mortgages, credit was a major stimulus for bank revenues; the market was expanding, and the interest rates paid by customers were high. The emergence of the financial crisis has shown the fragility of this model of development, highlighting at the same time the unsustainability of the revenues obtained by numerous players in those years; research work focusing on the crisis period mainly involves negative contributions from the share of loans out of total assets in the generation of profitability for banks. Also in this case, therefore, the control variable tends to have an unstable sign in the empirical works (see Demirgüç-Kunt and Huizinga, 2000; Abreu Mendes, 2001; Goddard et al., 2013).

For the second variable referred to above as a proxy of the business model, that is, interest income, at least in part, the considerations made with reference to the loan share are valid; in effect, one might expect to find a positive correlation between the two variables. The amount of interest income in the financial statements derives from the quantity and quality of the credit disbursed by the bank; about the quality issue, there are also competitive and macroeconomic factors that we will discuss later and that need to be taken into account. A bank focused on traditional retail commercial banking activities tends to have a significant share of interest income out of operating revenues; this makes it potentially very profitable in times of boom in the credit market, but also very fragile during periods of strong economic turbulence (among others, see DeYoung and Roland, 2001; Stiroh, 2006; Stiroh and Rumble, 2006; Calmès and Liu, 2009; Kok et al., 2015).

This latter aspect is linked to a theme related to the choice of business model, but often treated separately: that of revenue diversification (on this topic, see Carbo Valverde and Rodriguez Fernandez, 2007; Baele et al., 2007; Lepetit et al., 2008; Elsas et al., 2010; Calmès and Theoret, 2010; Sanya and Wolfe, 2011; Kohler, 2014; Kohler, 2015). Knowing that concentration of revenues on a single source of income exposes one to significant risks if an adverse scenario emerges (e.g. a serious economic crisis that makes the recovery of loans granted difficult, due to widespread default among customers), many banks may prefer to diversify revenue sources. This is indeed a strategic choice widely pursued by larger banks; today, many of the largest banking groups in Europe have numerous sources of revenue, ranging from lending to trading, from consulting to asset management. The idea underlying diversification of revenue sources is very simple and derives from the portfolio theory 'don't put all your eggs in one basket'; this is, in fact, a simple and effective risk management strategy. However, while in the field of investments diversification can be implemented at a low cost through the purchase of different financial assets, in the banking world this strategy appears more expensive and complex to carry out. The ability to activate effective revenue diversification processes is linked to a bank's ability to bear the costs related to the implementation of organizational processes, technological investments and the acquisition of skills for personnel assigned to new functions. It is clear that these dynamics require adequate adaptation time for the bank; in fact, it does not seem possible to pursue diversification strategies over a very short time, as is possible for financial stock picking. The cost to be paid can be high; the volatility generated by new sources of revenue may be greater than the beneficial effect of diversification deriving from the low correlation between the various activities carried out, leading to a loss for the bank. This is the so-called "dark side of revenue diversification" introduced in a famous article by Stiroh and Rumble (2006); in fact, to date, there is no unequivocal empirical evidence regarding the effect of revenue diversification on the level and stability of bank profitability.

While on the subject of loans and interest income, the role played by possible credit deterioration must, of course, be borne in mind; this is an aspect that emerged with great emphasis at the outbreak of the international financial crisis. The variables used in the literature in this regard are varied, and range from the share of non-performing loans out of total loans, troubled loans out of total loans or the level of loan loss provisions inserted by the bank in its income statement. As a rule, all these aspects have provided strong empirical evidence in explaining the dynamics of bank profitability; the expected sign of the coefficients associated with these variables is naturally negative (on this topic, see Bikker and Hu, 2002; Foos et al., 2010; Chronopoulos et al., 2015).

Another aspect that the severe international financial crisis has highlighted is the role played by a bank's regulatory capital level; as previously mentioned, the low level of many intermediaries' equity in the past allowed them to generate extremely high levels of ROE. However, the outbreak of the crisis highlighted the fragility of intermediaries characterized by excessively high levels of leverage, and prudential regulation intervened to limit these speculative strategies. Financial leverage (or capital ratio) has therefore become a particularly important explanatory variable in the field of empirical research (e.g. Dietrich and Wanzenried, 2014, Kok et al., 2015; IMF, 2017). Financially, a lower degree of financial leverage should be accompanied by a lower risk of default for the bank, and therefore its greater resilience even in the face of market turbulence. These aspects should contribute to reducing stakeholders' expected returns, facilitating the creation of value. However, it must be recalled that analysis using ROE as dependent variable may have a negative contribution from leverage, due to the presence of equity in the leverage numerator and the denominator of the ROE.

A serious issue deriving from the international crisis at the macroeconomic level is the sharp reduction in interest rates and the increase in competition between banks. In this context, a particularly significant factor in explaining the profitability gaps between banks has proven to be their level of efficiency; an ability to mask costs fails when gains become narrower. To this is added the fact that the presence of particularly high fixed costs (such as those borne to maintain wide-reaching branch networks) tends to make a bank's returns more volatile. The key variable widely used in the literature (among others, see Molyneux and Thornton, 1992; Goddard et al., 2013; Kok et al., 2015; IMF, 2017) is the cost income ratio, calculated as the ratio between operating costs and operating revenues; it is a particularly informative indicator, since it throws light whether a bank is able to balance recurring costs and revenues. Although there are entities able to operate with extremely low fixed costs, thanks to their structure (e.g. online banks or banks that operate through tied agent networks), as a rule, banks that carry out traditional activities and manage to reach a low cost income ratio tend to perform better than others. This is a variable that management itself should monitor with great care, partly in order to conduct effective benchmarking activities as regards competitors. It should be noted in this regard that the importance of the cost income ratio lies in its ability to compare costs and revenues, and not merely to provide a representation of the costs incurred. In other words, a limited cost income ratio can be achieved both through a reduction in costs and an increase in revenues; it is the relationship between the two which is significant. It follows that a policy of mere cost-cutting could prove to be completely mistaken where a reduction in charges leads to customer dissatisfaction with the service received, with consequent lower revenues in the future. The cost income ratio could even be reduced by increasing costs, offset, however, by proportionally higher revenues; it is undoubtedly one of the main indicators for understanding the ability of management to make virtuous choices for the bank's future.

Finally, other variables linked to specific governance characteristics can influence bank profitability; these may concern the nature of the bank (e.g. cooperative banks), its organizational structure (e.g. group membership) and the bank's governance, starting from the type and composition of the shareholders (see, for example, Iannotta et al., 2007). Extensive research has investigated these aspects, again leading to contrasting results depending on the survey context and the time period considered.

2.4.2 *External Determinants of Profitability*

Banks are crucial for the functioning of financial markets, but also of the economy as a whole; their nature as asset and risk transformers means they play a leading role in intermediation activities, coming into contact with companies, families, public administrations and other intermediaries. This results in a very close link between the life of a bank and the environment in which it operates; it is therefore normal that there is a very strong relationship between environmental factors and bank profitability. In the literature, the external determinants of bank profitability are generally divided into three categories: macroeconomic factors, competitive factors and regulatory factors.

Of the macroeconomic factors, the elements that appear to be most able to influence bank profitability are the economic cycle, the level of market interest rates and inflation.

The economic cycle is normally approximated through variations in gross domestic product (GDP); specifically, bank profitability is expected to follow a pro-cyclical trend (among others, see Athanasoglou et al., 2006; Beckmann, 2007; Albertazzi and Gambacorta, 2009; Goddard et al., 2011; Kanas et al., 2012; Kok et al., 2015; IMF, 2017). GDP growth should therefore stimulate banks' revenues, while the onset of recession leads to a reduction in income (often through an increase in non-performing loans due to customer default). Given that GDP performance tends to summarize all the surrounding economic conditions, and therefore the profit opportunities for companies operating on the market, this variable is present in most empirical research work.

Interest rate and inflation rate trends are other elements used frequently as control variables for the financial conditions of the economy. A reduction in interest rates is often accompanied by a decrease in a bank's profit margins; it is not by chance that the fall in rates observed after the outbreak of the international financial crisis has been indicated as a potential key element to explain the reduction in European bank profitability (see Claessens et al., 2016). As regards inflation, the same is partially true, since in this case too the focus is on the bank's ability to maintain an adequate level of marginality by passing on price increases through the rates offered and charged to customers. The sign linked to coefficients associated with both variables is therefore not univocally determinable a priori and requires empirical verification (Demirgüç-Kunt and Huizinga, 2000; Greenspan, 2004; Pasiouras and Kosmidou, 2007; Beltratti and Stulz, 2012; Trujillo-Ponce, 2013).

Competitive factors have long represented a key explanatory variable in bank profitability estimation models (e.g. Beck et al., 2006; Berger et al., 2009; Tregenna, 2009; Mirzaei et al., 2013); the ability of banks to benefit from monopolistic or oligopolistic returns was indeed an important element in not perfectly competitive markets. Even today, market competition is often included as a control variable in bank profitability, using proxies such as the Herfindahl Hirschman Index or the market share of the top 3, 5 or 10 banks. The traditional theories that deal with the effect of competition on firm profitability have been applied to the banking sector through different approaches. Among them, we can cite the S-C-P (Structure-Conduct–Performance) hypothesis, the Efficient-Structure hypothesis, the Expense Preference hypothesis and the Galbraith-Caves Risk-avoidance hypotheses (see Rasiah, 2010, for a review of literature on these topics). A higher degree of market concentration is usually associated with collusive behaviors, leading to oligopolistic rents. However, a concentrated banking market can also be the result of harsh competition between intermediaries: under this assumption, the final outcome can be a compression of banks' margins, reducing the overall profitability. As a result, the expected effect of concentration on profitability is uncertain.

Finally, regulation can play a decisive role in explaining a bank's ability to generate profits, for example, regulations that prohibit the bank from carrying out certain activities or, on the contrary, oblige banks to adopt certain competitive behaviors. In general, all banking regulation tends to affect the income opportunities of intermediaries, and therefore should be taken into account in cross-country surveys. From this point of view, the harmonization process that has affected the countries belonging to the European Union has considerably reduced over time the differences between state regulations; however, asymmetries remain in some areas (such as accounting) that could benefit some banks. It is very complex to include regulatory differences in a single variable; nonetheless, some attempts have been made, achieving a large following in research work (Barth et al., 2004).

2.5 Conclusions

After this analysis it should be clear that defining and measuring bank profitability is particularly complex and involves selecting appropriately from a huge number of financial indices (an interesting critical analysis of performance measures is provided in ECB, 2010). Indeed, the increasing sophistication characterizing data providers, financial statement reclassification processes and company evaluation models has generated a proliferation of financial ratios; thus, the analyst is obliged to make specific choices, opting for indexes with greater signaling value and greater interpretative content. The risk of an unsound choice is as obvious as it is relevant: the generation of misleading results. Note that this adverse outcome may be random (e.g. when the analyst chooses an index which is not appropriate for comparison, omitting some relevant information), or may sometimes be sought by the banks themselves (as in the case of those managers who work in such a way as to maximize the value of some bank indices known to be used by the market to make its own evaluations). The creation of appropriate best practices should prevent both of these situations; it is, however, the existence of such best practices that is being questioned.

For many years, bank profitability analysis focused mainly on measures linked to the level of income generated by banks; the emergence of crisis phenomena led to the discovery (or, in some cases, the rediscovery) of risk-adjusted measures, able to provide a more in-depth and correct view of bank profitability patterns. It is, however, desirable that a movement of research and debate on the most suitable metrics for measuring the performance of the banking sector, with regard to companies both listed and non-listed on regulated markets, be launched in the academic world and among regulatory and supervisory authorities and practitioners. In this direction, the road ahead is still long and in many respects unknown.

References

Abreu M., Mendes V. (2001), Commercial bank interest margins and profitability: evidence for Some EU Countries, Proceedings of the Pan-European Conference Jointly organized by the IEFS-UK & University of Macedonia Economic and Social Sciences, Thessaloniki, Greece, 17–20 May.

Albertazzi U., Gambacorta L. (2009), Bank profitability and the business cycle, Journal of Financial Stability, 5.

Athanasoglou P., Delis M., Staikouras C. (2006), Determinants of Bank Profitability in the South Eastern European Region, MPRA Paper No. 10274.

Baele L., De Jonghe O., Vander Vennet R. (2007), Does the Stock Market Value Bank Diversification?, Journal of Banking and Finance, 31.

Barth J. R., Caprio G. Jr., Levine R. (2004), Bank regulation and supervision: what works best?, Journal of Financial Intermediation, 13.

Beck T., Demirgüç-Kunt A., Levine R. (2006), Bank Concentration, Competition, and Crises: First Results, Journal of Banking and Finance, 30.

Beckmann R. (2007), Profitability of Western European banking systems: panel evidence on structural and cyclical determinants, Deutsche Bundesbank Discussion Paper, Series 2: Banking and Financial Studies No. 17/2007.

Beltratti A., Stulz R.M. (2012), The credit crisis around the globe: Why did some banks perform better?, Journal of Financial Economics, 105.

Berger A.N., Klapper L.F., Turk-Ariss R. (2009), Bank Competition and Financial Stability, Journal of Financial Services Research, 35.

Bikker J.A., Hu H. (2002), Cyclical patterns in profits, provisioning and lending of banks and procyclicality of the new Basel capital requirements, BNL Quarterly Review, 221.

Calmès C., Liu Y. (2009), Financial Structure Change and Banking Income: A Canada- U.S. Comparison, Journal of International Financial Markets, Institutions and Money, 19.

Calmès C., Theoret R. (2010), The Impact of Off-Balance-Sheet Activities on Banks Returns: An Application of the ARCH-M to Canadian Data, Journal of Banking and Finance, 34.

Carbo Valverde S., Rodriguez Fernandez F. (2007), The determinants of bank margins in European banking, Journal of Banking and Finance, 31.

Chronopoulos D.K., Liu H., McMillan F.J., Wilson J.O.S. (2015), The dynamics of US bank profitability, The European Journal of Finance, 21.

Claessens S., Coleman N., Donnelly M. (2016), Low-for-long Interest Rates and Net Interest Margins of Banks in Advanced Foreign Economies, IFDP Notes, Board of Governors of the Federal Reserve Board, Washington, DC.

Demirgüç-Kunt A., Huizinga H. (2000), Financial Structure and Bank Profitability, World Bank Policy Research Working Paper, no. 2430, August.

DeYoung R., Roland K.P. (2001), Product Mix and Earnings Volatility at Commercial Banks: Evidence from a Degree of Total Leverage Model, Journal of Financial Intermediation, 10.

Dietrich A., Wanzenried G. (2014), The determinants of commercial banking profitability in low-, middle, and high-income countries, The Quarterly Review of Economics and Finance, 54.

ECB – European Central Bank (2010), Beyond ROE – How to measure bank performance, Appendix to the report on EU banking structures, September.

ECB – European Central Bank (2018), SSM thematic review on profitability and business models, Report on the outcome of the assessment, September.

Elsas R., Hackethal A., Holzhauser M. (2010), The Anatomy of Bank Diversification, Journal of Banking and Finance, 34.

Foos D., Norden L., Weber M. (2010), Loan growth and riskiness of banks, Journal of Banking and Finance, 34.

Gambacorta L., van Rixtel A. (2013), Structural bank regulation initiatives: approaches and implications, BIS Working Papers, No. 412.

Goddard J., Molyneux P., Wilson J.O.S. (2004), Dynamics of Growth and Profitability in Banking, Journal of Money, Credit and Banking, 36.

Goddard J., Liu H., Molyneux P., Wilson J.O.S. (2011), The persistence of bank profit, Journal of Banking and Finance, 35.

Goddard J., Liu H., Molyneux P., Wilson J.O.S. (2013), Do Bank Profits Converge?, European Financial Management, 19.

Greenspan A. (2004), Risk and uncertainty in monetary policy, speech at the meeting of the American Economic Association, San Diego, CA.

Iannotta G., Nocera G. Sironi A. (2007), Ownership structure, risk and performance in the European banking industry, Journal of Banking and Finance, 31.

IMF – International Monetary Fund (2017), Spain: Financial Sector Assessment Report; Technical Note: Determinants of Bank Profitability, IMF Country Report No. 17/339, Washington, DC.

Kanas A., Vasiliou D., Eriotis N. (2012), Revisiting bank profitability: A semiparametric approach, Journal of International Financial Markets, Institutions & Money, 22.

Kohler M. (2014), Does Non-Interest Income Make Banks More Risky? Retail-Versus Investment-Oriented Banks, Review of Financial Economics, 23.

Kohler M. (2015), Which Banks are More Risky? The Impact of Business Models on Bank Stability, Journal of Financial Stability, 16.

Kok C., Móré C., Pancaro C. (2015), Bank Profitability Challenges in Euro Area Banks: The Role of Cyclical and Structural Factors, Financial Stability Review, Volume 1, European Central Bank.

Lepetit L., Strobel F. (2013), Bank insolvency risk and time-varying Z-score measures, Journal of International Financial Markets, Institutions and Money, 25.

Lepetit, L., Nys E., Rous P., Tarazi A. (2008), Bank Income Structure and Risk: An Empirical Analysis of European Banks, Journal of Banking and Finance, 32.

Mirzaei A., Moore T., Liu G. (2013), Does market structure matter on banks' profitability and stability? Emerging vs. advanced economies, Journal of Banking and Finance, 37.

Molyneux P., Thornton J. (1992), Determinants of European bank profitability: A note, Journal of Banking and Finance, 16.

Pasiouras F., Kosmidou K. (2007), Factors influencing the profitability of domestic and foreign commercial banks in the European Union, Research in International Business and Finance, 21.

Rasiah D. (2010), Review of Literature and Theories on Determinants of Commercial Bank Profitability, Journal of Performance Management, 23.

Sanya S., Wolfe S. (2011), Can Banks in Emerging Economies Benefit from Revenue Diversification?, Journal of Financial Services Research, 40.

Shehzad C.T., De Haan J., Scholtens B. (2013), The relationship between size, growth and profitability of commercial banks, Applied Economics, 45.

Smirlock M. (1985), Evidence on the (non)relationship between concentration and profitability in banking, Journal of Money, Credit, and Banking, 17.

Stiroh K.J. (2006), A Portfolio View of Banking with Interest and Noninterest Activities, Journal of Money, Credit, and Banking, 38.
Stiroh K.J., Rumble A. (2006), The Dark Side of Diversification: The Case of U.S. Financial Holding Companies, Journal of Banking and Finance, 30.
Tregenna F. (2009), The fat years: the structure and profitability of the US banking sector in the pre-crisis period, Cambridge Journal of Economics, 33.
Trujillo-Ponce A. (2013), What determines the profitability of banks? Evidence from Spain. Accounting and Finance, 53.

CHAPTER 3

Profitability of European Banks: A Quantitative Analysis

Abstract This chapter provides an analysis of profitability for a large sample of European banks since the onset of the recent severe international financial crisis. The asymmetries that continue to characterize the various European countries and the differences between the banks operating in them are highlighted. In particular, the analysis focuses on the determinants of bank profitability in Europe and aims to identify the drivers that support the production of positive and stable returns. The aim of the chapter is to identify some behaviors that can be considered as more virtuous, thus determining possible best practices that could serve as an example and guide for the banking sector.

Keywords Cluster analysis • Panel analysis • Crisis • Determinants of profitability • Competitive structure

3.1 Introduction

Providing an effective representation of the profitability profiles of the European banking system and of the determinants that have enabled the banks to achieve them is a complex exercise. We are dealing with a phenomenon that involves numerous intermediaries, characterized by business

M. Borroni, S. Rossi, *Banking in Europe*, Palgrave Macmillan Studies in Banking and Financial Institutions,
https://doi.org/10.1007/978-3-030-15013-6_3

models, efficiency, ownership structures, macroeconomic contexts and regulatory frameworks that are often very different from each other.

In the previous chapter, we outlined the main internal and external determinants of bank profitability. In that context, we observed that many of these variables, although generally significant in explaining the performance of a bank, do not always present a stable sign in estimation models. In the course of this chapter, we will use these variables to try to explain the behavior of European banks during the great international financial crisis. In particular, our analysis is aimed at identifying better models in terms of achieving more satisfactory levels (in degree and volatility) of profitability. The chapter is divided into three conceptual parts: in the first we analyze the macroeconomic and competitive context in which European banks operate; in the second we conduct a cluster analysis on a sample of European banks; in the third, this same sample is examined through a panel analysis in order to identify the main determinants of bank profitability during the great international crisis. The analysis focuses on the countries belonging to the European Union, by virtue of the key role that this political agreement plays in the overall European economy.

3.2 The Macroeconomic and Competitive Context of Reference

Banks and their local contexts have always tended to form symbiotic associations among themselves. It is not by chance that the trend of the economic cycle of a given country is a key variable for explaining its banking system's state of health (see Chap. 2); crisis phenomena tend to generate a significant deterioration in the quality of the credit portfolio, increasing non-performing loans and the overall business risk for the bank. Likewise, other financial aspects such as the trend in inflation rates, interest rates, risk premiums and demographic dynamics can have a significant influence on the bank's revenue margins and on its operational and organizational strategies. With reference to this last point, consider, for example, the issue of the closure of bank branches due to depopulation dynamics, such as those that occurred widely in the second decade of the twenty-first century in many rural areas.

These preliminary observations suggest that the existence of macroeconomic and regulatory differentials between countries can significantly influence the performance of the respective banking sectors; from this point of view, Europe does not seem to be an area characterized by homogeneous conditions at the local level. This affirmation remains true even where the geographical aspect is superseded in favor of a political interpretation of the links between countries, taking into consideration structured and intensive forms of economic integration such as the European Union and the European Monetary Union. Indeed, even within these associations between countries, there are numerous fundamental economic differences; the process of convergence toward fully phased models has not yet been completed and the existing asymmetries sometimes produce marked differences between macroeconomic variables from one country to another.

Figure 3.1 shows the data for variation in GDP for the countries of the European Union in two distinct time intervals; the first roughly covers the decade that preceded the great international crisis, while the second covers the period between 2009 and 2017.

Two distinctive elements emerge with great clarity. The first concerns the dramatic contraction in GDP growth rates observed following the outbreak of the crisis; overall, in the countries belonging to the European Union, the average figure fell from 2.3% to 0.8%, respectively, in the two subperiods examined (from 2.1% to 0.6% in the Euro Zone countries). This massive economic slowdown is one of the most serious and visible manifestations of the financial crisis; it led to the exit of numerous companies (industrial and banking) from the market, to phenomena of great instability in the financial sector and to changes in families' behavior in their investment and consumption choices.

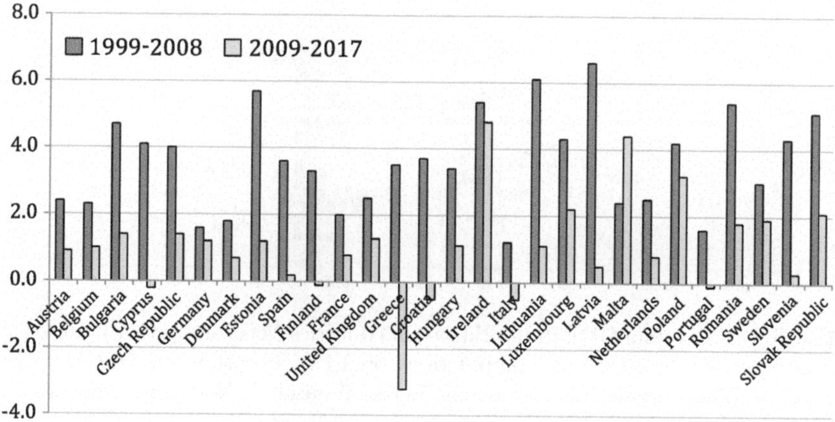

Fig. 3.1 GDP growth before and during the crisis. Source: ECB (2018)

The second element that can be derived from Fig. 3.1 is the considerable variability in growth rates characterizing the economies of the European Union; this, however, is true both in the period preceding the crisis and in the subsequent period. It is natural and foreseeable that economically less developed (or smaller) countries show higher rates of GDP variation in absolute terms than more developed economies; however, the data suggest that some potential outliers are developed economies such as Greece and Italy, which show a pronounced weakness in the time period considered in our analysis. At the same time, the comparative advantage of economies more oriented toward advanced financial services emerges, showing a capacity for greater resilience and recovery even after periods of severe turbulence. This is not the right place to discuss the suitability of GDP for describing the health status of an economy; however, it is clear that wide differences exist in the economic conditions of the countries examined.

Figure 3.2 elaborates on this analysis with reference to the per capita GDP dynamics; in particular, the data recorded at the end of 2017 (horizontal axis) are correlated with the rate of change experienced by the indicator itself in the period between 2009 and 2017 (vertical axis).

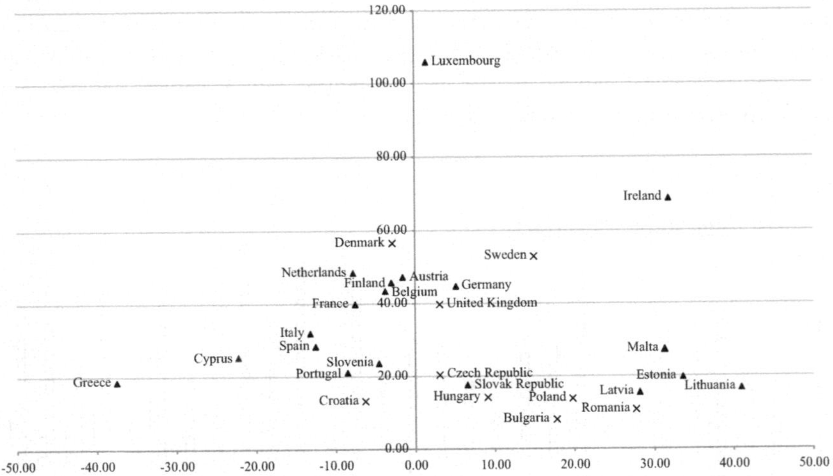

Fig. 3.2 Per capita GDP in the European countries (level and growth rate during the crisis). Source: Our computations on ECB, Eurostat and OECD data. Y-axis: GDP per capita (2017; current Euros, thousand); X-axis: growth rate of GDP per capita (2009–2017)

In this case too it is possible to observe how the so-called PIGS countries present problematic issues both in the absolute level and in the rate of variation experienced by per capita GDP; however, the dramatic decline by almost 40 percentage points seen in Greece (more than 42%, if the calculation is made with respect to the 2008 figure) clearly emerges. On the contrary, strong increases are registered by the new incoming countries in the Euro area, with the exception of Cyprus; for them, therefore, a beneficial process of convergence toward the fundamentals that characterize the first entrant countries has begun. Even ignoring Luxembourg and Ireland, which have per capita GDP values that are significantly above average, data dispersion is clear in Fig. 3.2, confirming the profound differences in the economic conditions of the countries surveyed.

Figure 3.3 shifts the focus to the theme of interest rates characterizing the members of the European Union. In particular, it relates the average inflation rate observed in the period 2009–2017 (vertical axis) to the average level of long-term rates of return over the same time frame (horizontal axis).

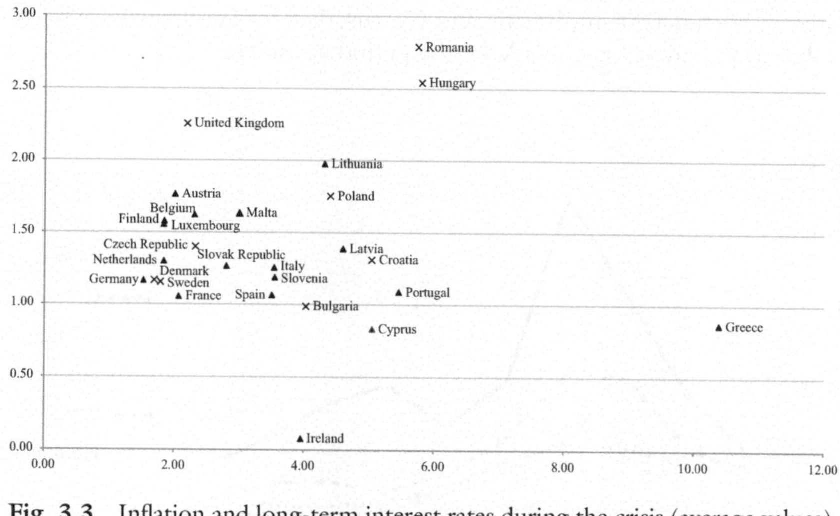

Fig. 3.3 Inflation and long-term interest rates during the crisis (average values). Source: Our computations on ECB and Eurostat data; average annual rates for each country (2009–2017). Y-axis: HICP; X-axis: Long-term interest rates (Long-term interest rate for convergence purposes—ten-year maturity)

While the level of inflation is one of the factors underlying monetary policy maneuvers, the long-term rate incorporates different risk premiums deriving from numerous factors, such as the market's perception of issuer soundness. Despite the fact that inflation is rather homogeneous in the countries considered, there are differences of some percentage points between the lowest and highest levels; the areas characterized by higher levels of inflation are outside the Euro Area. With reference to long-term rates, in Fig. 3.3, countries located at the left margin are generally characterized by a low issuer risk; on the contrary, Greece, isolated at the extreme right of the figure, once again stands out as a substantial outlier due to the enormous risk premiums that it was forced to pay off on its public debt. Although some extraordinary monetary policy operations have undoubtedly had a tangible effect on the containment of government bond yields, the differentials observed in Fig. 3.3 appear to be considerable.

It should be borne in mind that period averages tend to conceal a phenomenon of great importance in the area considered: the so-called European (sovereign) debt crisis, which originated around 2009, peaked in 2011, and was finally reduced in 2012. Figure 3.4 shows the average annual trend of long-term yields in the countries most involved, namely Greece, Portugal, Spain, Ireland and Cyprus; data for Germany have been added to provide a benchmark for the period considered.

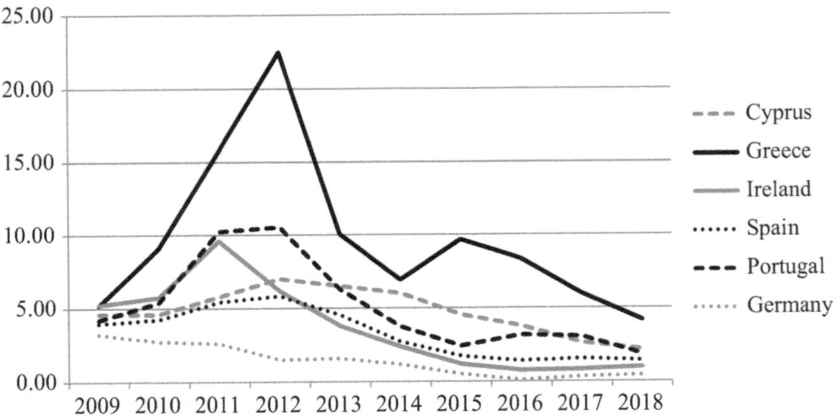

Fig. 3.4 Long-term interest rates during the crisis in selected countries. Source: Our computations on ECB data

What in fact was 'a crisis within a crisis' caused profound macroeconomic and financial imbalances, with dramatic implications for the banking sector both in the countries involved and in those more exposed to the failing economies. This happened for a number of reasons, including the large share of investments in government securities held by many banks: what is generally considered a low (or no)-risk investment suddenly became a highly volatile asset class with pronounced issuer risk. Once again, the data show that the European Union was a highly uneven area during the crisis/crises.

Similar results can be found by investigating another fundamental aspect among the determinants of bank profitability: the competitive and structural framework of the banking sector. Figure 3.5 shows the positioning of the countries belonging to the European Union according to the two main metrics with which the concentration of the banking industry is determined: the Herfindahl Hirschman Index (horizontal axis) and the shares of the first five credit institutions (vertical axis). Both indicators are constructed based on banks' total assets.

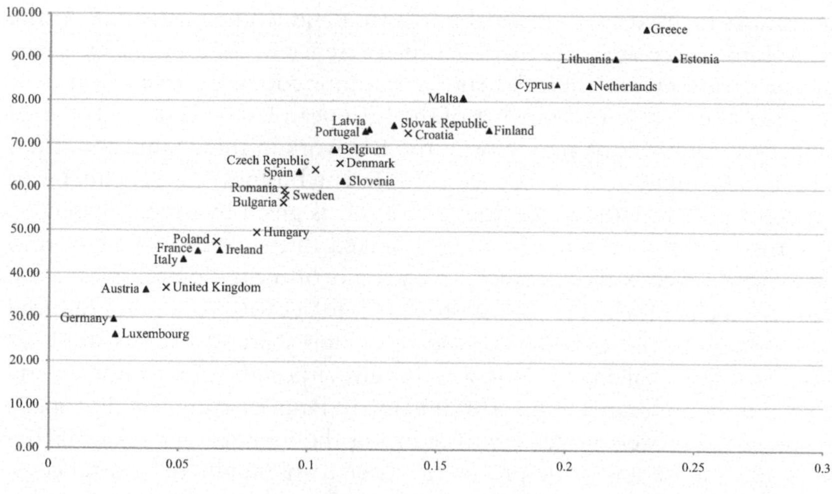

Fig. 3.5 Banking market concentration in the European countries (2017). Source: Our computations on ECB data. Y-axis: Share of total assets of five largest credit institutions; X-axis: Herfindahl index for credit institutions (based on total assets)

Besides the natural and expected positive correlation between the two indicators, Fig. 3.5 is characterized by strong data dispersion; the competitive dynamics in the countries of the European Union are therefore markedly different. Although the threshold traditionally considered critical for HHI of 0.25 is not exceeded, several countries exhibit moderate degrees of concentration; on the contrary, systems such as those in Germany and Luxembourg (but this could also include Austria, United Kingdom, Italy and France) show high levels of competitiveness.

These data indirectly reflect the number of operators in the European banking system; Table 3.1 illustrates the salient variables with reference to structural elements. In particular, the number of credit institutions, bank branches and bank employees of the countries belonging to the European Union are highlighted. To further underline the differences between countries, data on the number of branches per 100,000 inhabitants, the number of bank employees per 100,000 inhabitants and the number of employees per credit institution are also reported.

The result is a strongly uneven overall picture. Some countries are characterized by an extremely high number of banks; these are mainly economies in which there are many cooperative subjects, characterized by small size, strong roots in the local area through brick-and-mortar branches, businesses focused on traditional borrowing and lending activities. At the same time, there are cases in which the presence of local branches is particularly widespread; Table 3.1 shows that four countries have about two-thirds of the total bank branches of the European Union. Half of the total employees of the banking sector in the EU work in these same countries. These data suggest the existence of different business models linked to different cost structures. An example of this is given by models based on intensive physical presence in an area, linked to the banks' willingness to deal face-to-face with customers. As a result of technological innovation processes, changes in the ways customers interact with banks and reduced profit margins, these models (based on a high share of fixed costs) have been strongly challenged. Not surprisingly, although some countries still have number of branches per 100,000 inhabitants far above the European average, the process underway of reducing the number of bank branches is rapid, intense and widespread. In order to highlight the existence of further differences within the European Union, the penultimate column of Table 3.1 clearly shows the existence of some economies dedicated to financial business: Malta, Cyprus and Luxembourg have a very high share of banking sector workers with respect to the resident population.

Table 3.1 Structural statistics of the European banking system (2017)

	No. of Cis	*Branches*	*Employees*	*Branches (per 100,000 inhabitants)*	*Employees (per 100,000 inhabitants)*	*Employees × Cis*
Austria	572	3765	71,927	43	815	126
Belgium	88	3195	53,002	28	464	602
Bulgaria	27	3060	30,070	43	427	1114
Cyprus	35	460	10,632	53	1230	304
Czech Republic	55	1863	41,566	18	392	756
Germany	1632	30,072	597,319	36	721	366
Denmark	100	1007	42,240	17	731	422
Estonia	36	95	4920	7	373	137
Spain	206	27,480	183,016	59	392	888
Finland	267	970	20,999	18	381	79
France	422	37,209	398,516	55	593	944
United Kingdom	370	9690	353,299	15	533	955
Greece	38	2168	41,707	20	388	1098
Croatia	31	1118	20,434	27	498	659
Hungary	60	2417	38,877	25	398	648
Ireland	347	916	26,891	19	556	77
Italy	546	27,374	281,928	45	466	516
Lithuania	83	480	8922	17	318	107
Luxembourg	141	217	26,149	36	4344	185
Latvia	54	249	8492	13	439	157
Malta	25	102	4924	21	1035	197
Netherlands	92	1619	75,215	9	438	818
Poland	645	13,855	168,800	36	444	262
Portugal	141	4696	46,238	46	449	328
Romania	37	4596	55,044	24	282	1488
Sweden	156	1978	70,877	20	700	454
Slovenia	18	560	9844	27	476	547
Slovakia	26	1233	18,879	23	347	726

Source: Our computations on ECB and Eurostat data

All the data examined tend to confirm that the European Union (and the Euro area) includes countries characterized by marked differences in macroeconomic fundamentals, in growth processes and in the competitive variables typical of the banking sector. The crisis has undoubtedly helped to accentuate this phenomenon, introducing highly critical issues that have led some countries to experience painful adjustment: the Greek case is exemplary here. If the macroeconomic and competitive variables have an impact on the profitability of a bank, there is no doubt that the European Union countries provide different opportunities to the intermediaries operating within them.

3.3 Some Aggregated Data on the Subject of Bank Financials

Newspaper accounts of the great international financial crisis have covered many painful stories of bank failures; on the other hand, these are the most spectacular manifestations of a phenomenon of instability, those that often touch general public savers' interests more closely. Bank runs are without doubt the most widespread and sadly known testimony.

After providing an overview of the macroeconomic and competitive conditions that have characterized the European Union countries since the outbreak of the international crisis, in this short paragraph we want to focus on the reaction of bank balance sheets to these critical phenomena. To do this, we examine the aggregated data at the country level with reference to the main items of profitability, efficiency and quality of the loan portfolio; these are some of the key variables that have been identified in the literature (see Chap. 2) as useful for comprehending the health status of a bank and its ability to adequately remunerate capital.

Figures 3.6 and 3.7, respectively, dedicated to the ROA and ROE of the banking system, show bank profitability trends in the countries belonging to the European Union during the crisis. In particular, the data refer to the average ROA and ROE for the banks of each individual country during the period 2009–2017. The average value generated by the European Union banking system in the same period has been highlighted in black, in order to provide a meaningful benchmark.

The data confirm the previous analysis: the crisis has not hit the different countries of the European Union in the same way, and this is reflected in the profitability levels of the banking sector. It should be stressed that the crisis has undoubtedly depressed the overall profitability of banks operating in the European Union, but those that have suffered the most belong to the countries involved in the European (sovereign) debt crisis. Following the development of what could be defined as a 'perfect storm', the assets of European banks were first undermined by the deterioration in the quality of loans granted and subsequently hit by a rise in sovereign

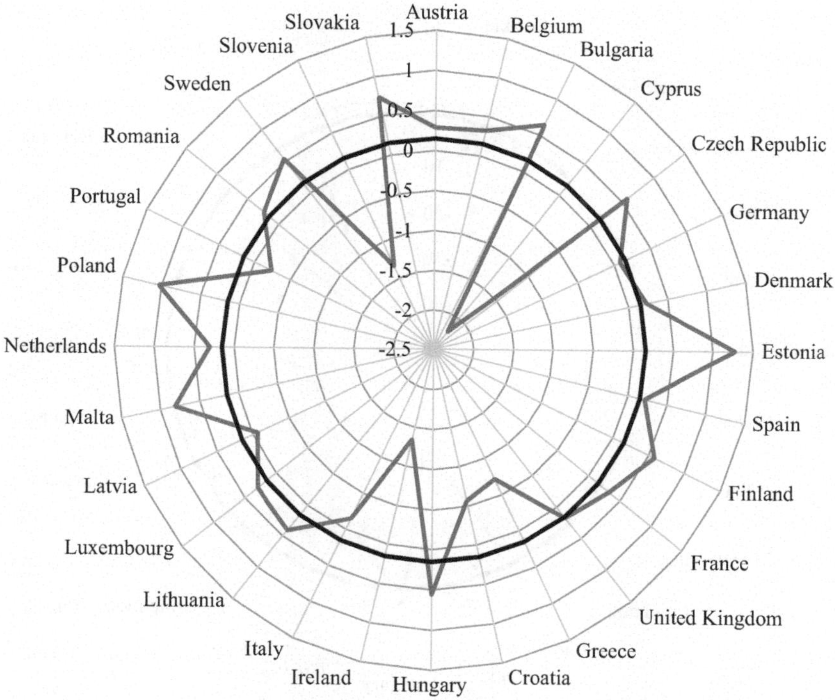

Fig. 3.6 Average ROAA of the banking system during the crisis (2009–2017). Source: Our computations on ECB and Eurostat data. In black: average ROAA of the EU banking system

risk, which reduced the value of numerous assets held in their portfolios. From this point of view, the values for Cypriot, Irish and Greek banks highlight the difficulties they faced; the data essentially reflect the macroeconomic turbulence already reported in the previous paragraph. It should be noted that although Figs. 3.6 and 3.7 are somewhat similar, their different shape signals a different leverage in the banking system of the countries investigated; this leads to a divergence of data in absolute values of ROE and ROA (the sign, which depends exclusively on the numerator of the two indicators, naturally remains the same).

Figure 3.8 calls into question another key variable in explaining the dynamics of bank profitability, that is, the degree of efficiency of the banks themselves. In particular, it is the cost income ratio, as stated in the previ-

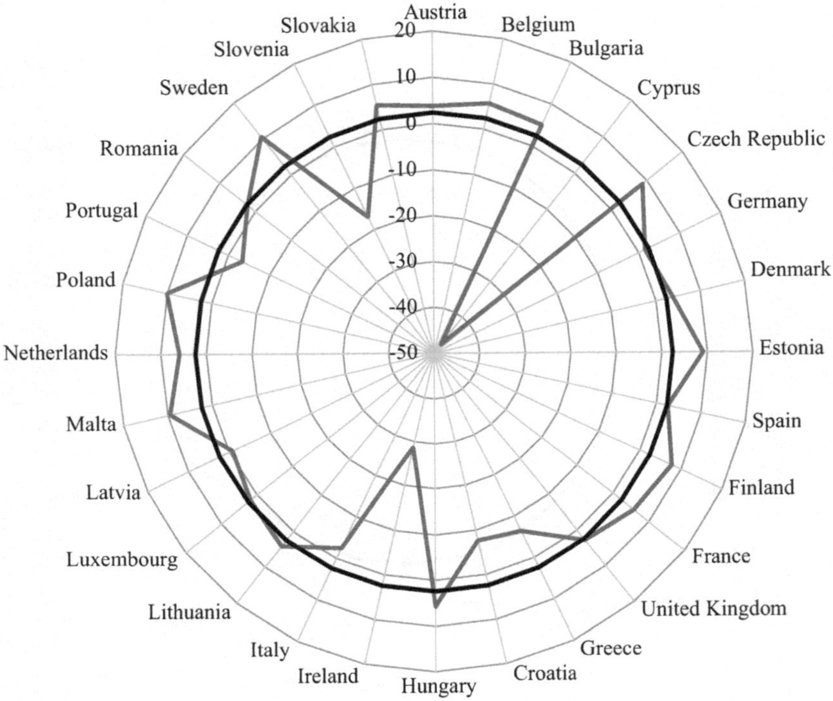

Fig. 3.7 Average ROAE of the banking system during the crisis (2009–2017). Source: Our computations on ECB and Eurostat data. In black: average ROAE of the EU banking system

ous chapter, that represents the most widely used metric in the literature to measure the efficiency of a bank.

Once again we observe a tangible dispersion of data around the average value found at the level of the European Union and represented in the figure by the black ring; the interpretation of the data compared to the previous figures must naturally be the opposite, with the most virtuous cases located at levels below the average. However, there is an underlying weakness in degree of efficiency in three of the main banking systems of the European Union and of the Euro Area itself (Germany, France and Italy); in these countries, it is no coincidence that massive restructurings are being carried out to rationalize local branches in order to reduce the incidence of fixed costs on revenues.

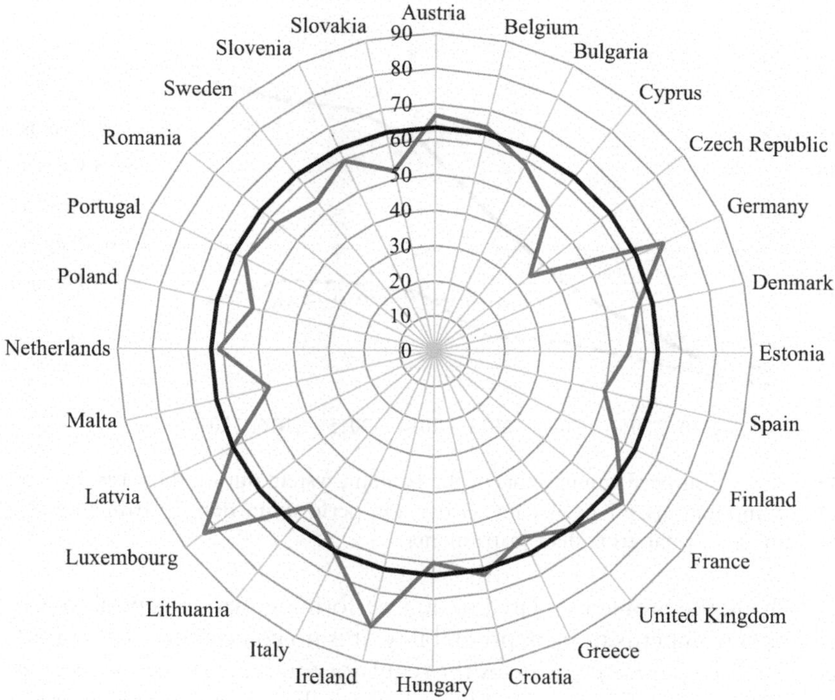

Fig. 3.8 Average cost income ratio of the banking system during the crisis (2009–2017). Source: Our computations on ECB and Eurostat data. In black: average cost income ratio of the EU banking system

Another component that the crisis has highlighted as a key element in determining a bank's profitability and risk is the quality of the loan portfolio. In fact, the great international crisis itself was born as a credit crisis, and its spread through the economy led to an acceleration of default processes in companies in different sectors. In a context such as the European one where the traditional model of commercial banking prevails, this led to the deep wounds in the banking sector that attempts are laboriously being made to cure. Figure 3.9 shows the dynamics of non-performing loans (as a share of total loans) in some countries that have proved particularly exposed to the problem of 'bad debt'; the average value registered at European Union level has also been included as a benchmark.

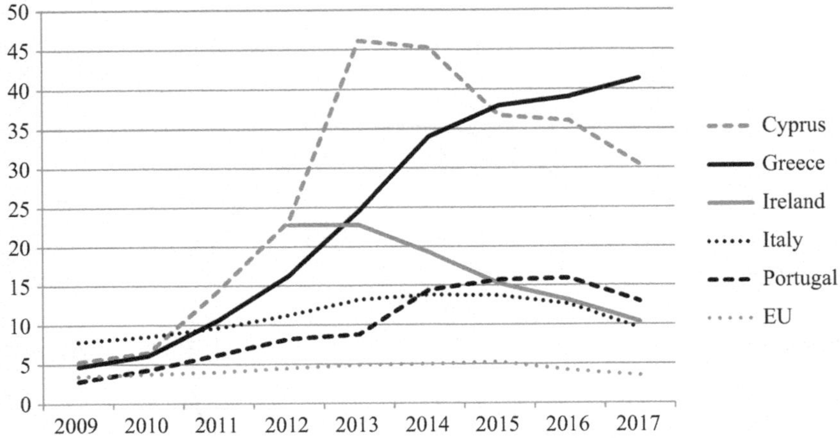

Fig. 3.9 Non-performing debts of the banking system during the crisis. Source: Our computations on ECB data. Gross non-performing debt instruments as a percentage of total gross debt instruments

Solving the problems related to non-performing loans is central to providing new impetus to bank profitability; it is no coincidence that considerable efforts have been made by the regulatory and supervisory authorities to create support for the sale of these balance sheet items and the identification of best practices for the management of problem loans (EBA, 2018). The data show that for some countries, the process of convergence toward the European Union average has not yet begun, while for others, the gap is still extremely wide, despite some progress since the most acute phases of the crisis.

More in general, observation of aggregate country-level data on profitability, efficiency and credit quality of the respective banking systems tends to confirm the indications provided by macroeconomic analysis. Very different country systems still exist; convergence, at least at the level of banking systems, has therefore not yet been achieved.

This exploratory analysis of the data requires further appropriate investigations, aimed at clarifying the causal links explaining the creation of bank profitability in the years of the great international financial crisis. In the next two paragraphs, we will proceed in this direction, passing from the country-level to bank-level analysis.

3.4 European Banks During the Crisis: Cluster and Panel Analyses

In order to perform a quantitative analysis regarding the determinants of profitability and risk-adjusted profit measures for the European banking sector during the recent financial crisis, we built a wide dataset including bank-level and macroeconomic information. The source of income statement and balance sheet data was SNL Market Intelligence. More specifically, the sample included only entities classified as 'banks' or 'cooperative/saving' banks in the SNL database; consolidated data were preferred to individual financial statements. We focused on the banks located in the countries belonging to the European Union, observed for the period 2009–2017. The geographical scope of our sample allowed us to reduce the asymmetries between countries as regards the regulatory and legal framework; at the same time, the time span under scrutiny made it possible to explore the behavior of the banks during the harshest moments of the global crisis and the following recovery period.

Macroeconomic and competitive figures were collected from different sources: specifically, the ECB, Eurostat and OECD. Since we are interested in the risk-return profile of European banks, the analysis made use of some simple measures of risk, such as the standard deviation of bank returns. In order to reduce the negative impact of missing data in computing these figures, we applied some filters to the data: specifically, for the cluster analysis, we required the presence of a full set of data for each bank-year observation, while for the panel regressions, we required the presence of at least seven years of available data. We performed several checks in order to eliminate outliers, misclassified banks, individual banks incorporated in groups already included in the dataset and entities involved in significant M&A processes. The final sample was made up of 205 banks, of which 101 were included in the cluster analysis; Table 3.2 outlines the sample composition (see Sect. 3.4.2 for a comment about the presence of a large number of French banks in the sample; UK banks are not included in the cluster analysis due to some missing macroeconomic data).

Table 3.3 lists and describes the variables used in the following sections. For a deeper analysis of them (and for detailed references), see the previous chapter.

Table 3.2 Sample composition

Country	*Panel analysis*	*Cluster analysis*
Austria	13	3
Belgium	4	
Bulgaria	1	
Czech Republic	2	2
Denmark	10	5
Finland	4	2
France	57	40
Germany	35	18
Ireland	1	
Italy	27	13
Luxembourg	2	1
Malta	3	1
Netherlands	5	2
Poland	6	5
Portugal	5	1
Romania	1	
Slovakia	3	
Slovenia	1	
Spain	7	5
Sweden	3	3
United Kingdom	15	
Total	*205*	*101*

3.4.1 Cluster Analysis

In this study, we aimed to identify peer groups of banks that performed differently during the great financial crisis. The focus of the analysis was on discriminating between banks that can be considered as more 'virtuous' and banks that paid a high price in terms of (low) profitability during the period under consideration. In order to provide a dynamic view of the European banks' behavior, we split the time span under scrutiny into three different periods: the first covering the sovereign debt crisis (2009–2011), the second the immediate aftermath period (2012–2014) and the third the following recovery period (2015–2017). For each of these subperiods, we estimated the mean value of several variables outlined in Table 3.3. In particular, after a preliminary Principal Component Analysis, we included in the cluster analysis the following variables: ROAA, ROAE, NIM, size, interest share, cost income, capital, problem loans, GDP, LTIR, SH5.

Table 3.3 Description of variables

Type	*Variable*	*Measure*
Dependent variables	ROAA	Net income/average total assets
	ROAE	Net income/average total equity
	NIM	Net interest margin
	RAROAA	ROAA/σROAA
	RAROAE	ROAE/σROAE
	Z-Score	(ROAA + tangible equity/tangible assets)/σROAA
Bank-specific independent variables	Size	Natural logarithm of total assets
	Interest share	Net interest revenues/operating revenues
	Loans share	Net loans/total assets
	Deposit share	Customer deposits/total assets
	Capital	Tangible equity/tangible assets
	Problem loans	Problem loans/gross customer loans
	Cost income	Operating expenses/total revenue
	Asset growth	Annual growth of total assets
Macroeconomic independent variables (country level)	GDP	GDP growth
	HICP	Inflation (Harmonized Index of Consumer Prices)
	LTIR	Long-term interest rate
	SH5	Share of total assets of five largest credit institutions

The strategy of using mean values reduces volatility in balance sheet items and provides a medium-term vision of bank results. Due to the peculiar features of the time span under consideration, the dataset included several extreme observations; to reduce these, we trimmed the data for some variables (ROAA, ROAE, NIM, interest share, capital, asset growth) at the 5-percentile level for each tail.

From a methodological point of view, we used a weighted pair-group method based on arithmetic averages as a clustering algorithm over the sample. This approach allowed us to obtain differently sized clusters; moreover, it took into account the characteristics of each bank within the groups, highlighting data dispersion within the cluster. This approach was applied to the three subperiods under scrutiny; Calinski–Harabasz pseudo-F was used to define the optimal number of clusters. The outcome of this

Table 3.4 Cluster analysis (2009–2011, mean values)

	Cluster 1	*Cluster 2*	*Cluster 3*	*Cluster 4*
ROAA	0.63	0.46	0.28	0.29
ROAE	7.43	7.37	4.10	3.98
NIM	1.66	2.16	1.76	1.85
Size	17.50	17.33	17.15	16.74
Interest share	54.31	69.07	70.85	61.16
Cost income	55.05	58.80	60.14	71.80
Capital	8.59	6.18	6.10	6.91
Problem loans	3.42	6.74	6.11	5.53
GDP	0.49	−0.45	0.52	0.05
LTIR	3.67	3.67	3.12	4.09
SH5	47.86	71.99	31.83	41.84
Number of banks	*40*	*13*	*23*	*25*

process is presented in Tables 3.4, 3.5, and 3.6, which include the number of banks included in each cluster and the average figures of the variables of interest for each peer group.

Table 3.4 shows the features of the four clusters of banks defined for the period 2009–2011, that is, during the sovereign debt crisis. As previously affirmed, that period was a 'perfect storm' that severely affected the European banking system, already weakened by the effects of the subprime crisis.

The first cluster includes 40 banks that, during the period under examination, achieved fully satisfactory income results, as witnessed by the highest ROAA and ROAE levels of the entire sample. These banks are medium to large in size, have a high degree of efficiency, as evidenced by a low level of cost income ratio, and have a high level of regulatory capital. At the same time, they managed to contain the level of problem loans: the quality of their loan portfolios (and the presence of income fund diversification) is also visible by observing the data of NIM and the interest income share of operating revenues, both lower than those found for the other clusters.

The second cluster includes 13 banks that share several statistics with the peer group described above; in this case too, the profitability results were good and the average size large, and the level of efficiency appears satisfactory. However, these banks presented data indicating a greater focus on interest income; the higher level of NIM and problem loans highlight the impact of macroeconomic variables on the banks' business, especially with reference to the provision of loans to customers. Alongside

Table 3.5 Cluster analysis (2012–2014, mean values)

	Cluster 1	*Cluster 2*	*Cluster 3*
ROAA	0.63	0.50	0.29
ROAE	6.54	7.45	4.13
NIM	1.70	1.97	1.69
Size	17.26	17.49	17.27
Interest share	57.31	64.10	62.97
Cost income	53.56	58.98	65.43
Capital	10.12	6.61	7.06
Problem loans	3.85	6.99	6.19
GDP	0.42	0.61	0.42
LTIR	2.74	2.24	2.37
SH5	48.66	74.04	39.58
Number of banks	34	12	55

Table 3.6 Cluster analysis (2015–2017, mean values)

	Cluster 1	*Cluster 2*
ROAA	0.72	0.45
ROAE	10.10	4.87
NIM	1.78	1.52
Size	18.25	17.17
Interest share	61.44	56.26
Cost income	54.77	64.31
Capital	6.78	9.20
Problem loans	4.09	5.24
GDP	3.02	1.75
LTIR	0.94	0.93
SH5	68.06	41.55
Number of banks	21	80

the negative figure in GDP growth, this cluster of banks shows high market concentration, signaled by the value of the SH5 variable that is much higher than that of the other groups of banks.

The third cluster groups 23 players, with profitability data clearly lower than those previously described. In this case, disadvantageous elements are summed together: a strong propensity for interest income, a lower degree of efficiency, a high proportion of bad loans, a lower level of regulatory capital. It should be noted that this occurred in the presence of better macroeconomic conditions compared to previous clusters, thanks to higher GDP growth and a lower level of long-term interest rates.

The fourth and last cluster includes 25 banks; these are the subjects that, on average, recorded lower levels of profitability during the sovereign debt crisis. These are smaller banks with a level of cost income ratio clearly greater than that of the other banks in the sample. Despite having a fairly diversified operating income composition, they suffered the adverse macroeconomic conditions through an increase in NIM, together with a deterioration in the quality of loan portfolios. These are banks that are more closely linked to local areas, with a significant brick-and-mortar presence that determines an increase in the cost structure, and therefore are more directly affected by local macroeconomic problems.

Table 3.5 shows data for the period 2012–2014, for which the clustering model adopted suggests the creation of three groups of banks.

The first cluster includes 34 banks; as before, these are the subjects that performed better overall in the period examined. These banks showed a fairly high profitability level both in terms of ROAA and ROAE; these data are well explained by the distinctive features that can be observed in the other variables. In fact, the banks in the cluster in question had high levels of efficiency, a high level of regulatory capital, a low presence of problem loans and a lower share of interest income on operating revenues. These elements were able to mitigate the presence of more problematic macroeconomic variables compared to the banks belonging to the other two clusters.

The second group of banks includes 12 banks that achieved satisfactory overall profitability; the high level of ROAE found, moreover, is partially explained by the lower level of regulatory capital that characterized these intermediaries. Compared to the previous cluster, there was a higher level of bad loans, accompanied by an NIM higher than that observed for the other groups. However, a satisfactory level of efficiency, which tended to compensate for weaknesses in the credit sector, came to the rescue of these banks.

The third cluster includes 55 banks, with profitability profiles significantly lower than those found for the banks described above. Observation of Table 3.4 shows the high level of the cost income ratio found on average for the banks in this subsample; it is accompanied by a high proportion of interest income, a lower level of regulatory capital than the most virtuous group and a high share of bad loans. It should be noted that during the period under review, the macroeconomic variables began to improve widely, and therefore banks' microeconomic peculiarities tended to emerge; the banks that did not improve their efficiency and did not clean out the non-performers in their loan portfolios paid the price for this delay.

Table 3.6 shows the data for the period 2015–2017 for the two clusters of banks suggested by the clustering algorithms.

The first observation that can be made concerns an element which is cross-sectional to the two groups of banks: there was a clear improvement in macroeconomic variables, signaling the start of a process of return to normal after the terrible years of the great international crisis. GDP growth tended to accelerate, while long-term interest rates returned to low levels.

The first cluster includes 21 banks that achieved high profitability when compared to the immediately preceding years. These players were characterized by a high level of efficiency, a low share of problem loans and a macroeconomic framework that certainly supported the creation of value.

The second cluster of banks reveals lower profitability levels; specifically, they had a higher level of regulatory capital, greater diversification of revenue sources and a smaller average size.

Overall, the breakdown of the period of observation into subperiods permits appreciation of the constancy of some elements as the context conditions change. More specifically, despite the undoubted influence of macroeconomic dynamics in explaining the income results of a bank, the examination of European banks carried out and described in this paragraph suggests that the efficiency and the quality of the loan portfolio are the basis of a policy for profitability promotion. We can even affirm that the presence of these two attributes manages to compensate, as far as is possible, an adverse macroeconomic scenario; at the same time, they allow the bank to accelerate its performance during economically more prosperous periods.

3.4.2 Panel Analysis

In order to increase the depth and robustness of the previous analysis, in this paragraph we perform panel regression estimation on the data of the banks in our sample. The estimated equation is as follows:

$$\Pi_{it} = \alpha \Pi_{it-1} + \sum_{j=1}^{J} \beta_j X_{it}^{j} + \sum_{m=1}^{M} \beta_m X_{it}^{m} + c_t + \varepsilon_{it}$$

where Π_{it} is the dependent variable (i.e. profitability or risk-adjusted profit of bank i at time t), c_t is the constant term and ε_{it} the disturbance term; explanatory variables are grouped into bank-specific $\left(X_{it}^{j}\right)$ and macroeconomic $\left(X_{it}^{m}\right)$.

As dependent variables, we use three profitability metrics (ROAA, ROAE and NIM) and three metrics for risk-adjusted returns (RAROAA, RAROAE and Z-Score). RAROAA and RAROAE were built by reporting the ROAA and the ROAE with the respective levels of standard deviation over the whole period considered; this means that the denominator is the same for all the years of observation, while the numerator changes on the basis of the data observed in that specific year. Z-Score is calculated as the sum of the ROAA and the equity-to-asset ratio, divided by the standard deviation of the ROAA. In particular, following Lepetit and Strobel (2013), we use the average level of the ROAA over the whole period under scrutiny to calculate the numerator of the index; the standard deviation of the ROAA is calculated over the whole time period too.

As stated previously, the presence of extreme macroeconomic and microeconomic phenomena in the period under analysis determined the presence of numerous borderline observations. Hence, in this case too, we trimmed the data for some variables (ROAA, ROAE, NIM, interest share, capital, asset growth, as we did for the cluster analysis) at the 5-percentile level for each tail.

Table 3.7 shows the descriptive statistics of the variables included in the econometric analysis.

Given that dynamic specification introduces problems of consistency, in order to estimate the dynamic panel model properly, we relied on instrumental variable techniques such as GMM estimators (Arellano and Bond, 1991; Blundell and Bond, 1998). Both GMM-DIF and GMM-SYS estimator have been tested; the following tables report results using Blundell and Bond (1998) specification; however, sign and significance of the coefficients associated to the covariates do not change using different models.

Further tests have been performed using fixed-effects dynamic panel regressions and excluding French banks, since they numerically dominate the sample outlined in Table 3.2; main results are not affected by these robustness checks (detailed results are available on request).

Table 3.8 shows the results of the econometric estimation for profitability measures.

Table 3.7 Descriptive statistics

Variable	*Observations*	*Mean*	*Standard Deviation*	*Minimum*	*Maximum*
ROAA	1770	0.38	0.38	−1.48	1.48
ROAE	1745	4.84	4.99	−23.05	16.06
NIM	1782	1.70	0.63	0.46	3.79
RAROAA	1594	3.06	2.41	−0.55	9.57
RAROAE	1571	2.89	2.09	−0.56	8.15
Z-Score	1447	56.10	36.54	13.04	151.76
Size	1801	17.27	1.67	13.09	21.54
Interest share	1774	61.92	12.67	34.11	102.22
Loans share	1801	65.24	14.43	19.15	93.09
Deposits share	1800	52.79	18.22	5.04	92.57
Capital	1786	7.42	2.95	2.44	14.95
Problem loans	1582	5.70	3.74	1.53	17.57
Cost income	1777	62.58	10.71	33.56	94.06
Asset growth	1723	1.82	6.08	−15.33	21.56
GDP	1818	0.91	2.42	−8.27	25.12
HICP	1818	1.32	1.11	−1.70	6.10
LTIR	1818	2.42	1.59	0.09	10.55
SH5	1818	46.81	14.34	25.01	89.73

As expected, the results found for the regressions concerning the ROAA and the ROAE have similar coefficients for sign and statistical significance. In the period under review, some microeconomic factors and macroeconomic variables played an important role in explaining the profitability of the European Union banks. Indeed, the econometric estimates indicate negative and significant coefficients for cost income ratio and the share of problem loans out of total loans. Therefore, it was the more efficient banks with healthier credit portfolios that achieved the best results. The coefficient associated to the interest share is significant in all the regressions; however, it changes sign in NIM estimate, as we will see later. This outcome is coherent with the behavior of the dependent variables described in the previous chapter; the same can be said about the changing sign of the coefficient associated to the capital.

The role of macroeconomic variables emerges when addressing banks' profitability. GDP growth is associated with a positive and highly significant coefficient, confirming the pro-cyclical nature of bank profitability. Moreover, a positive and significant coefficient for the variable measuring the degree of concentration of the market is observed.

Table 3.8 GMM regression (profitability measures)

Variables	*(1)*	*(2)*	*(3)*
	ROAA	*ROAE*	*NIM*
Dependent$_{t-1}$	0.26***	0.17***	0.59***
	(0.029)	(0.027)	(0.031)
Size	0.03***	0.21	0.01
	(0.010)	(0.148)	(0.008)
Interest share	−0.00***	−0.08***	0.01***
	(0.001)	(0.014)	(0.001)
Loans share	−0.00***	−0.03**	−0.00
	(0.001)	(0.015)	(0.001)
Deposits share	0.00***	0.06***	0.00***
	(0.001)	(0.010)	(0.001)
Capital	0.03***	−0.27***	0.03***
	(0.006)	(0.083)	(0.005)
Problem loans	−0.02***	−0.37***	0.01***
	(0.003)	(0.048)	(0.003)
Cost income	−0.01***	−0.21***	−0.01***
	(0.001)	(0.020)	(0.001)
Asset growth	0.01***	0.06**	−0.01***
	(0.002)	(0.025)	(0.001)
GDP	0.02***	0.34***	0.01**
	(0.004)	(0.059)	(0.004)
HICP	−0.01	−0.16	−0.02***
	(0.007)	(0.105)	(0.006)
LTIR	0.00	−0.01	0.04***
	(0.006)	(0.087)	(0.006)
SH5	0.00***	0.03***	0.00
	(0.000)	(0.006)	(0.000)
Constant	0.74**	20.53***	−0.54**
	(0.301)	(4.308)	(0.245)
Observations	1301	1266	945
Number of banks	201	201	195
AR1	*0.000*	*0.000*	*0.000*
AR2	*0.446*	*0.324*	*0.786*

This table presents the effects of bank-specific and macroeconomic covariates on profitability ratios. Bank-specific covariates have been used in GMM-style instruments; macroeconomic controls have been included in standards (exogenous) instruments. Robust standard errors in parentheses. Significance codes: *** indicate statistical significance at 1%, ** at 5% and * at 10%

As for the NIM, different results are recorded. Since this is a variable that tracks the raw level of profitability deriving from interest, several variables contribute to its dynamics, with different signs compared to those observed with reference to ROAA and ROAE. Consider, for example, the level of the long-term interest rate, as well as the degree of impairment of the loan portfolio, both conditions that tend to raise the general level of the rates applied. The coefficient associated with the interest share of operating revenues, which tends to highlight the bank's specialization in traditional lending activity, is also positive and statistically significant.

Note that all the three regressions report a positive and significant coefficient associated to the share of customer deposits on total assets; during a period characterized by relevant problems in the interbank market, the presence of a stable source of financial resources (moreover, with a cost directly set by the banks) has played a virtuous role in improving profitability.

Table 3.9 outlines the results of the econometric estimation for risk-adjusted performance measures.

The outcomes appear on the whole to be stable, with reference to the sign of the coefficients associated with the various explanatory variables in ROAA and ROAE estimates; instead, the absolute values of the coefficients change, as, in some cases, does their degree of statistical significance. Z-Score shows sometimes different links with the covariates selected for this analysis; this is not surprising, if we consider the great changes the occurred in the capital structure of the banking system during the time span under scrutiny.

In particular, size is associated with negative coefficients in ROAA and ROAE regressions; smaller banks therefore experienced better risk-adjusted profitability results. Likewise, in the same estimates, better bank performance was achieved with a lower share of interest income out of operating revenues; the ability to activate other forms of income therefore constituted a virtuous element in the ability to create value in times of crisis. Once again, efficiency and quality of the loan portfolio prove to be key variables in explaining the pattern of income results of the European Union banks. Similar confirmation comes from the observation of the coefficients associated with GDP growth, which are always positive and strongly significant.

Table 3.9 GMM regression (risk-adjusted profitability and stability measures)

Variables	*(1)*	*(2)*	*(3)*
	RAROAA	*RAROAE*	*Z-Score*
$Dependent_{t-1}$	0.43***	0.42***	0.97***
	(0.031)	(0.033)	(0.029)
Size	−0.16***	−0.29***	−0.37
	(0.047)	(0.052)	(0.267)
Interest share	−0.02***	−0.03***	0.06***
	(0.005)	(0.004)	(0.025)
Loans share	−0.00	0.00	−0.04*
	(0.004)	(0.004)	(0.026)
Deposits share	0.01*	−0.00	0.01
	(0.003)	(0.003)	(0.018)
Capital	−0.01	−0.14***	0.09
	(0.025)	(0.027)	(0.145)
Problem loans	−0.09***	−0.08***	−0.04
	(0.017)	(0.015)	(0.087)
Cost income	−0.05***	−0.04***	−0.07**
	(0.006)	(0.006)	(0.031)
Asset growth	−0.00	0.00	−0.33***
	(0.008)	(0.008)	(0.042)
GDP	0.05**	0.05***	0.01
	(0.020)	(0.019)	(0.146)
HICP	−0.13***	−0.14***	0.18
	(0.036)	(0.035)	(0.192)
LTIR	−0.03	−0.04	0.18
	(0.031)	(0.031)	(0.179)
SH5	−0.00	0.01**	−0.03**
	(0.002)	(0.002)	(0.011)
Constant	9.00***	11.51***	10.21
	(1.421)	(1.517)	(7.783)
Observations	946	894	762
Number of banks	182	183	160
AR1	*0.000*	*0.000*	*0.000*
AR2	*0.499*	*0.812*	*0.512*

This table presents the effects of bank-specific and macroeconomic covariates on risk-adjusted profitability ratios. Bank-specific covariates have been used in GMM-style instruments; macroeconomic controls have been included in standards (exogenous) instruments. Robust standard errors in parentheses. Significance codes: *** indicate statistical significance at 1%, ** at 5% and * at 10%

Z-Score regression shows a positive and significant coefficient associated to interest share; this result may be surprising. However, smaller banks focused on traditional commercial banking activities showed higher level of regulatory capital during the crisis; this could have led to this regression result. In this line can be read the negative coefficient associated to the growth rate experienced by the banks' assets; on the contrary, cost income ratio confirms its negative impact on profitability and risk-adjusted measures. Among macroeconomic covariates, only the concentration rate is associated with a significant coefficient; the negative sign seems to suggest the existence of a greater fragility due to the oligopolistic nature of the market.

Overall, the panel estimates outlined here confirm and strengthen the indications deriving from the cluster analysis conducted previously. Although the macroeconomic environment plays a key role in explaining the banks' profitability dynamics, some variables under the control of top management play a decisive role in guiding the observable profitability in financial statements. The greater resilience shown by the U.S. banks compared to their European counterparts after the most acute phase of the great international crisis has often been attributed to their ability to diversify business lines, increase efficiency by changing their organizational and competitive structure and improve the quality of their loan portfolios. The analyses conducted here seem to be confirmed by these indications, tracing a clear line that European banks must try to adopt as soon as possible.

3.5 Conclusions

Overall, the panel estimates outlined here confirm and strengthen the indications deriving from the cluster analysis conducted previously. Although the macroeconomic environment plays a key role in explaining the banks' profitability dynamics, some variables under the control of top management play a decisive role in guiding the profitability observable in financial statements. The greater resilience shown by the U.S. banks compared to their European counterparts after the most acute phase of the great international crisis has often been attributed to their ability to diversify business lines, to increase efficiency by changing their organizational and competitive structure and to improve the quality of their loan portfolios.

To be precise, many of these strategies require, simultaneously, adoption by the bank of suitable organizational and managerial choices, and the presence of appropriate background factors in the macroeconomic and regulatory framework. In this regard, we recall the differences existing at the international level in the development of financial markets, facilitating the pursuit of remunerative policies for diversifying a bank's activities, or the existence of rules and figures ready to support banks in the recovery of NPLs.

However, in the sample of European banks examined in this chapter, the search for efficiency, together with a progressive reduction of bad debts, represents the key elements for recovering profitability. Even so, the profitability levels observed before the financial crisis may never again be achievable by the banking sector in the future. Somewhat cynically, it could be said that the crisis itself brought on the cost-cutting process that the banking sector had postponed in the past, as the result of particularly high profit margins largely able to mask inefficiencies in organizational processes and management. Now, in a context of greater competition and lower profitability, many issues have come to the forefront and require the making of incisive, but wise, managerial choices.

References

Arellano M., Bond S. (1991), Some tests of specification for panel data: Monte Carlo evidence and an application to employment equations, The Review of Economic Studies.

Blundell R., Bond S. (1998), Initial conditions and moment restrictions in Dynamic Panel Data models, Journal of Econometrics, 87.

EBA – European Banking Authority (2018), Guidelines on management of non-performing and forborne exposures, 31 October.

ECB – European Central Bank (2018), Annual report 2017, 9 April.

Lepetit L., Strobel F. (2013), Bank insolvency risk and time-varying Z-score measures, Journal of International Financial Markets, Institutions and Money, 25.

CHAPTER 4

Making Profits in the New Competitive and Regulatory Framework

Abstract This chapter aims to identify the main guidelines by which the new competitive, regulatory and macroeconomic context can be translated into managerial behaviors capable of generating a sustainable level of profitability for the bank. The competitive pressure deriving from new entrants into the market, the macroeconomic environment characterized by lower growth and lower interest rates, the choice of the business model and the composition of a bank's assets are, in fact, strategic choices on which that bank's life depends. The chapter provides managerial 'instructions' in each of these areas of interest, starting from the data provided by the market examined in the previous parts of the book.

Keywords Business model • Management strategies • Costs • Capital • Stability • Bank branches

4.1 Introduction

It will be many years before all the effects generated by the financial crisis that broke out at the end of the last decade can be defined. However, all those who, in any capacity or to any degree, are part of the financial system, or have dealings with it, agree on one thing: the way of doing banking

M. Borroni, S. Rossi, *Banking in Europe*, Palgrave Macmillan Studies in Banking and Financial Institutions,
https://doi.org/10.1007/978-3-030-15013-6_4

has changed fundamentally, and we are unlikely to see a return to the past. Of course, the 'essence' of banking remains the same: taking deposits and granting loans. The need for a trusting relationship between the bank and its depositors also remains unchanged, a relationship that can be undermined even by simple rumors or fake news, with barely imaginable consequences, as the memorable scene of the bank run from 'Mary Poppins' effectively illustrates.

What has radically altered is the very nature of banking, whatever the causes (globalization, technology, etc.). What has not changed is the need to carry out this activity in a profitable way, and to do it in sustainable terms in the medium/long term.

4.2 The Quest for Profitability After the Great Crisis: A Proactive Approach

After almost a decade of management strategies influenced to a large extent by regulatory decisions, it is essential that credit institutions be finally able to define directions for development over extended time horizons in complete autonomy and with objective judgment.

Certainly, many regulatory or socioeconomic obstacles limit the degree of autonomy of the banker: in the financial sector, the mass sacking of personnel is a rare event, which normally occurs only in case of a bank's resolution; the substantial stagnation of the real estate market, and in particular commercial real estate, partly induced by the incredible development of online commerce, prevents banks from disposing of their branch networks without incurring serious losses; the tumultuous succession of new supervisory norms and rules, and the almost immediate alignment that the market requires, hinder the definition of clear and unequivocal strategic lines by credit institutions, and generate significant costs incurred in the ensuring of prompt adjustment.

It is precisely the somewhat difficult macroeconomic context that calls for a proactive approach by banks: now that the 'external' difficulties have been resolved or at least effectively curbed, they need to find solutions for those of a microeconomic nature, in particular, the issue of management costs and their careful and effective reduction. The recovery of operating efficiency represents one of the most important competitive challenges facing European banks, especially with respect to those in the U.S.A. (Feng and Wang, 2018), in order to ensure a rapid return to adequate levels of profitability.

At least three solutions could be adopted to achieve this challenging goal: a decisive rationalization of the branch network, a greater use of technology and the initiation of a consolidation process. Profound change of the branch network is not a simple operation and requires the bank to make difficult choices, sometimes not always feasible in complete autonomy: there may be impediments of a regulatory, environmental and sociodemographic nature that curb actions to reduce the number of existing branches. The business model widely adopted by European banks, oriented to retail, with typically deposit-gathering branches and a low added value per individual transaction, has always involved the need for numerous points of contact with clients, unlike more markedly wholesale models, which generate larger margins and do not require a great number of branches. With the exception of the Nordic countries, Europe has always suffered from an efficiency gap, even when there is a strong investment banking component. Assuming that the costs attributable to the branch network are approximately equal to a quarter of the operating costs, the International Monetary Fund has recently calculated that the closing of one-third of bank branches could result in an increase of five basis points in income after tax, and the Euro area even overtaking the U.S.A. If European bank branch networks were to reach the average level of deposits achieved by Nordic bank branches, the reduction in costs would more than double, with equally evident advantages in terms of income. The Monetary Fund recognizes that the application of this metric is only indicative because it ignores the differences in system structures between the various countries, the heterogeneity of the banks' business models and the costs associated with the closures that would be incurred (IMF, 2016). It is, however, an instructive theoretical exercise, as it permits identification of potential improvements in operational efficiency, achievable through a bold program of structural reforms.

A similar concern has also been expressed for some years now by the European Banking Authority (EBA), which has put operating expenses under observation as an element for assessing banks' ability to improve their levels of profitability. Although EU banks have continued to streamline their costs, progress in this direction has turned out to be rather modest: in 2017, the European Banking Authority noted that "on an aggregate basis, and by focusing only on variables controlled by banks, at the current yield banks would reach the break-even point between net interest income and operating expenses only with an average decrease of costs of 6.2%; in the last 12 months, costs decreased by 0.8%" (EBA, 2017). The main concerns are in the 'staff expenses and other administrative expenses' category: while the other administrative expenses could be justified by necessary adjustments induced by growing competition from fintech firms, the reduction in staff expenses appears rather 'sticky', as if indicating an inability by banks to adjust their cost structure at a pace similar to that with which changes in demand (financing and banking services) and the economic environment occur (EBA, 2018a).

The 'compulsory choice' to reduce branches involves a more and more marked use of technology by the bank, both to guarantee transactional rapidity and precision, and to meet changing clientele behavior. The latter is now typical of almost all European countries, albeit to different degrees of intensity, largely due to factors that are economic-structural (the widespread presence of technologically advanced networks, incentives for their increasing use, etc.) and sociodemographic (mainly age and education) (Fig. 4.1).

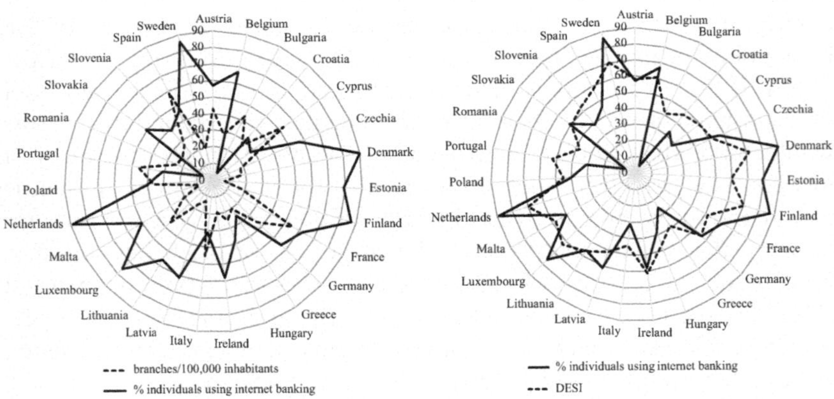

Fig. 4.1 Bank branches rationalization processes and internet banking diffusion in some European countries. Source: Eurostat, EU Commission (2017 figures). Left panel—number of bank branches per 100,000 inhabitants and percentage of individuals using the internet for banking (1). Right panel—percentage of individuals using the internet for banking and DESI (Digital Economy and Society Index). Notes: in the right panel, the Digital Economy and Society Index is a composite index that summarizes relevant indicators on Europe's digital performance and tracks the evolution of EU member states in digital competitiveness; it is calculated as the weighted average of five dimensions: connectivity, human capital, use of the internet, integration of digital technology and digital public services

Analysis related to the degree of digitalization of banking services underlines benefits and obstacles: while it is true that initial investments in information technology (IT) are decidedly high, both for acquiring the technology itself and above all for the necessary security that it entails, it is also true that in the medium to long term it will generate not only a significant reduction in costs (in terms of buildings, human resources, management, etc.) but also higher revenues, especially for leading companies, thanks to the acquisition of new customers. A recent analysis has shown that the impact of IT spending on bank profitability is positive but of varying intensity, to a certain extent, partly dependent on the degree of bank solidity: the more fragile the budget structure appears, the lower the investment in technology and, as a consequence, the benefits that could be derived from it. Alongside typically bank-specific obstacles, there may also be additional country-specific brakes: a low level of technological infrastructure development and a limited level of expertise among the population are further causes of delay in a bank's decision to invest which can only be overcome by means of targeted policies, in the absence of which credit institutions risk falling into a sort of 'profitability trap' (Huljak et al., 2018).

There is one further method of reducing costs, which is not generally welcomed by banks (and bankers) but is largely desired by supervisory authorities: cost savings can be obtained through merger and acquisition (M&A) processes. In the banking sector, M&A transactions can be undertaken for a number of reasons, such as reducing costs and achieving economies of scale, or expanding into growing markets, exploiting funding synergies and diversifying risks. Obstacles can instead be encountered in the form of regulatory or supervisory barriers, or by market and, above all, geopolitical uncertainties.

After a peak toward the end of the last century, and stabilization before the global financial crisis, the number of M&A transactions has slowed considerably, with overall values reduced. The cause of this downturn could be associated with a decline in the price valuations of bank shares; it is also true that the improvement observed at the end of the crisis period was not accompanied by a sharp recovery in merger and acquisition operations. Volumes and the number of transactions, which remained fairly contained both internally and even more so cross-border, seem to reflect the lack of opportunities for expansion and the perception of uncertain net benefits (Schmitz and Tirpak, 2017). While operations at the national level tend to be more driven by restructuring possibilities, those of a cross-border nature seem to be more focused on growth opportunities and more profitable banks. The long period of crisis has depressed M&A activity in Europe in recent years: persistent asset quality problems and lack of clarity in regulatory policy on NPLs in the Euro area, only recently resolved after a controversy between the ECB and European Commission (ECB Banking Supervision, 2017a, 2018; EU Commission, 2018; EU Council, 2018), have made it quite difficult to verify the feasibility of operations.

A certain reluctance by 'strong' banks to the start of transactions is justified by the high volatility that characterizes the banking equity market. In an 'ordinary' business cycle, disappointing profits and ever-increasing costs would surely be the trigger to carry out acquisitions, achievable cost synergies justifying merger premiums. The uncertainty of the geopolitical situation and weak expectations in terms of increased interest rates at the European level induce caution, but it is inevitable that consolidation is a strategy that the banking system will undertake; overbanking, undercapitalization, inefficiencies in the management of costs, as well as the repeated and pressing exhortation by regulatory authorities (IMF, 2017; Nouy, 2017; Draghi, 2018) and market expectations (Hildebrand, 2018; UBS, 2018) represent the main drivers pushing in this direction.

4.3 Reshaping the Business Model

One factor that undoubtedly affects profitability is the choice of organizational model through which the bank carries out its business: on this depends not only the composition of the income produced and its persistence over time, but also, as we have seen in recent decades, the bank's resilience to changing macroeconomic conditions and the introduction of significant structural changes in the financial system. In defining the model, an important role is played by the significant technological innovations that have led credit institutions to change their structural and operational organization radically over recent decades. To this should be added the growing level of competitiveness induced by a prolonged period of deregulation, the creation of the integrated single market in financial services (via the European Second Banking Directive) and the introduction of the euro. It is true that while wholesale markets have experienced an effective and high level of integration, retail banking and small business lending have still remained largely confined within national borders, with rather limited cross-border operations (Molyneux, 2013).

Deregulation and financial innovation have produced significant changes in bank business models: for example, securitization techniques, by allowing transition from an 'originate to hold' model, typical of traditional credit intermediation, to an 'originate to distribute' model, have effectively reduced banks' perception of risk, significantly altering the very nature of a bank (Ayadi et al., 2011). These changes have been reflected in numerous aspects of banking operations: the quest for greater size, achieved through the creation of large groups; the use of different funding methods, above all favoring market-based options; business diversification, with the aim of achieving economies of scope and less dependence on forms of interest income; changes in the corporate governance of the company. The consequence has been the creation of large banks, very diversified, but not for this reason 'different' from each other: as highlighted by Haldane (2009), "diversification strategies by individual firms generated a lack of diversity across the system as a whole". This may not be particularly significant from a micro-prudential perspective, but could have worrying consequences from a macro-prudential point of view in the event of a very severe aggregate shock.

The onset of the crisis, which originated in the financial field but then spread rapidly to the real economy, with heavy repercussions especially in some European countries, generated a profound reflection on banks' strategic and organizational solutions adopted up to that time, and on their ability to modify and/or adapt their business model to the changed socioeconomic context. A broad debate has thus developed at academic and regulatory levels (among others, FSA, 2009; Altunbas et al., 2011; Ayadi et al., 2012; ECB, 2016; Cosma et al., 2017; Di Antonio, 2018), to try to understand if and how different bank-specific characteristics, attributable to the various business models adopted, can permit early identification of hidden risks, which often occur only in the long run or when a systemic shock occurs. In particular, one of the business models that was most affected not only by the crisis but above all by the long continuation of a macroeconomic environment characterized by low interest rates was that of the traditional retail bank, in which the net interest margin, namely the difference between interest charged on loan transactions and that paid out on various forms of savings, represents the main component of profitability.

For European banks, the awareness of a need to rethink their business model arose following the introduction of the SREP, the Supervisory Review and Evaluation Process, whose first guidelines were published in 2014. The outcome of the assessment represents the up-to-date supervisory view of a bank's risks and viability. There are four areas of analysis the authorities submit to periodic evaluation: the bank's business model, internal governance and institution-wide control arrangements, risks to capital and adequacy of capital to cover these risks and risks to liquidity and adequacy of liquidity resources to cover these risks.

The business model has thus entered fully into the system of periodic evaluations that regulators have put in place (Fig. 4.2), albeit according to a principle of proportionality, which groups institutions in categories according to their systemic importance and intensity of cross-border activities. Obviously the model remains a bank's strategic choice, but it has started to represent an important element in assessment of its own and the entire credit system's stability: "Without undermining the responsibility of the institution's management body for organizing and running its business, the focus of the business model analysis (BMA) should be the assessment of the viability of the institution's current business model and the sustainability of its strategic plans. This analysis should also assist in revealing key vulnerabilities facing the institution that may be revealed by other elements of the SREP. Competent authorities should score the risk to the viability of an institution stemming from its business model and strategy keeping in mind that the aim of the BMA is not to introduce supervisory rating of various business models" (EBA, 2014).

The importance recognized by the regulators of the business model has contributed to further development of the line of studies that, for some years now, has recommenced analysis of the potential and risks of the various bank business models following significant changes in the macroeconomic context and competitive scenario of reference, their performance in terms of profitability and operating costs and, of course, their degree of resilience to the new macro-financial environment. Two approaches are usually adopted by researchers: the first involves the identification of the various bank business models based on predefined criteria, generally referable to one or more key balance sheet or income statement variables, lower or higher than a given percentage (size, loans, deposits, degree of specialization, etc.) (Bonaccorsi di Patti et al., 2016; Ayadi et al., 2016); the second, more widespread, is instead typically data-driven and uses statistical clustering techniques, based on one or more bank-specific indicators that represent a proxy for banks' business strategies (for example, loans to customers as a share of total assets, interbank funding as a share of total liabilities or net interest margin as a share of operating income). Once the different clusters of similar banks have been obtained, their performance is

To understand the means and methods used by an institution to operate and generate profits, competent authorities should undertake quantitative and qualitative analyses.

Quantitative analysis
Competent authorities should undertake an analysis of the quantitative features of the institution's current business model in order to understand its financial performance and the degree to which this is driven by its risk appetite being higher or lower than peers.
Areas for analysis by competent authorities should include:

a) profit and loss, including trends: competent authorities should assess the underlying profitability of the institution (e.g. after exceptional items and one-offs), the breakdown of income streams, the breakdown of costs, impairment provisions and key ratios (e.g. net interest margin, cost/income and loan impairment). Competent authorities should consider how the above items have evolved in recent years and identify underlying trends;
b) the balance sheet, including trends: competent authorities should assess the asset and liability mix, the funding structure, the change in the total risk exposures amount (TREA) and own funds, and key ratios (e.g. return on equity, Core Tier 1, funding gap). Competent authorities should consider how the above items have evolved in recent years and identify underlying trends;
c) concentrations, including their trends: competent authorities should assess concentrations in the P&L and balance sheet related to customers, sectors and geographic areas. Competent authorities should consider how the above items have evolved in recent years and identify underlying trends; and
d) risk appetite: competent authorities should assess the formal limits put in place by the institution by risk type (credit risk, funding risk, etc.) and its adherence to them in order to understand the risks that the institution is willing to take to drive its financial performance.

Qualitative analysis
Competent authorities should undertake an analysis of the qualitative features of the institution's current business model in order to understand its success drivers and key dependencies.
Areas for analysis by competent authorities should include:

a) key external dependencies: competent authorities should determine the main exogenous factors that influence the success of the business model; these may include third-party providers, intermediaries and specific regulatory drivers;
b) key internal dependencies: competent authorities should determine the main endogenous factors that influence the success of the business model; these may include the quality of IT platforms and operational and resource capacity;
c) franchise: competent authorities should determine the strength of relationships with customers, suppliers and partners; this may include the institution's reliance upon its reputation, the effectiveness of branches, the loyalty of customers and the effectiveness of partnerships; and
d) areas of competitive advantage: competent authorities should determine the areas in which the institution has a competitive advantage over its peers; these may include any of the above, such as the quality of the institution's IT platforms, or other factors such as the institution's global network, the scale of its business or its product proposition.

Fig. 4.2 SREP: quantitative and qualitative features of a bank's business model. Source: EBA (2014). In 2018 the European Banking Authority has revised the SREP framework: there has been no change in bank business model assessment guidelines

analyzed for different aspects, including, above all, profitability, efficiency and risk (ECB, 2016; De Meo et al., 2016; Bonaccorsi di Patti and Palazzo, 2018). However, this second approach, which has now become mainstream, is not exempt from clear limitations: first of all, it should be remembered that "cluster analysis is not an exact science" (Ayadi et al., 2016). Second, the identification of different business models through purely statistical techniques can be useful for providing certain information, but does not allow the drawing of definitive and absolute conclusions, since the results are heavily conditioned by the chosen variables, the quality of the underlying data and the geographic area investigated. Furthermore, for a more accurate assessment, these classifications should also incorporate relevant qualitative information, normally not available in public databases. Indeed, the data-driven approach often forgets that "business models are not one-dimensional", as the economic and financial variables chosen in the analysis could lead to the hypothesis: "simple labels, such as 'retail bank' or 'investment bank', do not adequately describe the business model of a bank and its performance and riskiness. Business models are diverse along different key dimensions" (Liikanen, 2012).

Finally, it should be borne in mind that business models change over time: the persistence of a difficult macroeconomic environment, characterized by modest levels of growth and the emergence of numerous outbreaks of crisis in the various financial systems, as well as by growing and pervasive regulation, has induced many credit intermediaries, especially in Europe, to change their strategic-organizational model to return to more traditional business (Roengpitya et al., 2014). However, behavior has not been uniform: "It is worth emphasizing that these broad observed changes to bank business models are far from fully consistent across the global banking sector. While many banks have significantly adjusted their business models, some have been able to broadly maintain their profile and activities (in part reflecting lower pressure for change), while others have even "swum a little against the tide" (CGFS, 2018).

Analyzing different bank business models, with their peculiarities and their strengths and weaknesses, is not the intention of this work; for these aspects, we refer to the wide and specialized literature available (above all, see Llewellyn, 2013; Ayadi, 2019). Here, it should be stressed that whatever the strategic-organizational solution adopted by a bank, it inevitably reflects on the composition and the amount of its profits. Empirical investigations conducted over the past few years have struggled to identify a "winning" business model, or at least one which performs better than the others; alongside the methodological difficulties outlined earlier, it is extremely difficult to identify a banking business model that ensures effective and persistent advantages in the economic-financial field.

Banks now operate in an extremely changeable context, where the speed and depth of the changes make it rather difficult to outline a long-term business plan: organizational structures quickly become obsolete, traditional operational paradigms change and regulation itself struggles to outline a precise framework, due to the onset of new risks, not necessarily originated within the financial system (e.g. cyber risk). At the same time, we need to deal with the legacy of the recent past: wrong investment choices and, in some cases, episodes of misconduct have left a structure of operating costs that is difficult to downsize and which seriously affects the profitability of the bank, sometimes rendering it negative or, at best, sluggish.

Against such a complex and unstable background, a further element of concern is represented by the impetuous growth of the fintech phenomenon which, although generated outside the traditional circuits of credit intermediation, is rapidly and significantly occupying one of the most traditional sectors: the payment system, which, up to a few decades ago, was the exclusive domain of banks. The retail commercial bank model, which has traditionally relied on a supply represented to a large extent by personal and saving accounts, linked to substitute instruments of legal tender (credit and debit cards, bank transfers, etc.), is openly 'challenged' by new and innovative non-bank competitors. These are quickly replacing banks in payment circuits, giving rise to two important consequences. The first, of a micro-prudential nature, is an increase in the level of competitiveness in the payment system, drastically reducing profit margins for banks and, consequently, the overall level of profitability (Siciliani, 2018). The second, macro-prudential, consequence is more complex because of the dilemma it poses to regulators. Money deposits, and the digital wallet payment services connected to them, find their *raison d'être* in the absolute trust of depositors in the possibility of their transformation into legal tender, immediately and without any costs. If a commercial bank is in trouble, the central bank can provide liquidity support to avoid its insolvency, or to secure all of its deposits, as was the case for Northern Rock in 2007 (Cunliffe, 2017). Should this ring-fencing also be extended to non-bank operators who provide payment services? And with what limits? Supervisors and supervisory bodies at international level have long been working on these issues (for an analysis of the main issues and implications for central banks and other authorities, see CPMI, 2014).

The framework outlined above justifies the targeted insistence by regulators (ECB Banking Supervision, 2017b; PRA, 2018) on business model characteristics and on the ability of banks to adapt to the new landscape, on profitability drivers and on the consequences they may have for banks' overall riskiness, to which many factors contribute (ECB Banking Supervision, 2017c). "The role of supervisors, in our view, is to assess and challenge business models, but not to control banks' development of their strategies and the corresponding business model. To be a bit more specific, the main objective of business model analysis is to allow competent authorities to develop a view on two main areas. Firstly, they should have a view of the current business model of the supervised institution, and its viability. Secondly, they should understand how the business model may evolve as a result of strategic choices made by the institution and/or the impact of changes to the business environment in which it operates and, therefore, its risks and sustainability" (Farkas, 2018).

4.4 The Quest for Equilibrium Between Profitability and Compliance to the Regulation

A decade after the dramatic onset of the international financial crisis, the main objectives of the regulatory reforms put in place to deal with it and guarantee stability to the banking system have largely been achieved: capital requirements have been raised, the quality of bank capital has improved, measurement of the risk level inherent in different banking activities has improved, excessive variability in the definition of risk-weighted assets has been reduced, the degree of leverage has been limited, measures to contain the degree of liquidity have been introduced and macro-prudential elements, which previously were almost entirely absent, have been incorporated into the regulation (BCBS, 2017).

Reform has thus strengthened the degree of resilience of the banking system; however, although it was widely agreed upon, none of the regulators is sure a 'first best' outcome has been achieved, especially from a medium- to long-term perspective. The complexity of the rules has often generated interpretative difficulties, which have then been reflected in different implementations in practical application, generating the opposite effect to that desired by the spirit of the norm, that is, uniformity of treatment in different situations. Even among regulators, there are those who feared creating "a regulatory Frankenstein's monster that no-one has full control over" (Ingves, 2014).

A challenge facing regulators is therefore that of close control and careful assessment of the degree of effectiveness of the new rules. It should not be forgotten that more than a decade of repeated and ever more pervasive regulatory changes, with the resulting reporting obligations, have given rise to a significant increase in the costs of adaptation to the new rules, to which are added those deriving from further regulatory adjustments and which include compliance costs, costs for the adaptation of computer systems, costs for staff training and the direct costs of supervisory authorities (supervisory fees). There are no recent estimates of the overall extent of the charges that the continuous evolution of regulation imposes on supervised subjects; in the past, some academic works focused on this subject, but limiting analysis to certain types of banks (for example, U.S. commercial banks; Elliehausen, 1998), or only to listed banks (Pasiouras et al., 2009), and without reaching unequivocal conclusions. Recently, in order to measure regulatory production, and indirectly its cost, some indicators have been used empirically, such as the growing number of publications by the main regulatory bodies (Coen, 2016), the high number of technical and organizational requirements imposed on the subjects monitored by the new regulatory provisions (KPMG, 2016, Deloitte, 2018) and the incremental share of costs sustained by banks for regulatory compliance projects (Moody's, 2018). In European countries, the creation of the Banking Union has added a further element of complexity in the definition and adjustment of each member state's regulatory system; as an example, the cost of supervisory fees alone increased by over 40% between 2015 and 2018 (source: ECB Banking Supervision).

Alongside the direct and indirect costs generated by the continuous production of regulations, at least two other factors must be considered that have negative repercussions on a bank's income statement. The first, which in the coming years should progressively decrease in impact, is constituted by non-performing exposures (NPLs). The difficulty, if not impossibility of their collection, has caused the supervisory authorities to 'impose' on banks a minimum mandatory deduction of their amount, or their sale to third parties (at 'sale prices', due to accelerated sales processes) over a limited number of years (ECB Banking Supervision, 2017a, 2018), compared to those discretionally adopted in the past. For banks that operate in economic systems widely financed by credit intermediation, this decision has led to the inclusion in their income statements of heavy losses on loans, with a clear weakening of profitability levels.

The second element is represented by the higher risk premium paid by credit institutions for raising capital on the market, especially that needed to meet the additional requirements to strengthen gone concern capital, in the form of minimum requirements for own funds and eligible liabilities (MREL) and total loss absorbing capacity (TLAC); both are forms of debt capital, aimed at providing banks with capital resources capable of absorbing losses and of restoring primary capital, or of allowing an orderly resolution. Since they are hybrid forms of risk capital and rank at the bottom of the capital repayment hierarchy, the remuneration required by the market, and therefore the cost that the bank must bear, increase directly in proportion to a perceived increase in the degree of overall bank risk.

If higher costs are inevitably reflected in a bank's income statement with a strong negative impact on its profitability, it must nevertheless be considered that a return to positive economic results does not necessarily enable the bank to ensure remuneration to its shareholders. Indeed, over recent years, numerous and repeated 'requests' have been made by supervisory authorities, invoking very prudent distribution of dividends (and, to an even greater extent, of the variable part of management remuneration) to avoid impacting on a bank's ability to establish and maintain a solid capital base, "to enable them to continue to fulfill all requirements and outcomes of the SREP even in the case of deteriorated economic and financial conditions" (for the most recent version, see ECB Banking Supervision, 2019). It is true that the recommendation is addressed to significant supervised entities and significant supervised groups, but it is also true that national authorities actually replicate this measure of moral suasion with regard to all credit institutions operating in the European Banking Union. Concern among bankers is evident: the fear of future crises is far from being eliminated, and, therefore, if against higher costs the risk of systemic instability still remains very high, with the well-known potential negative economic repercussions that derive from it, one wonders who benefits from a complex and expensive regulatory system that may not be able to 'grasp' the warning signs of a crisis and stem its inevitable consequences while, at the same time, disappointing the market and investors in terms of return on capital.

Another important aspect springs from these issues, concerning at least from a strictly numerical point of view the majority of European banks, that is, the proportionality of the rules. This is not a new topic for European banking regulation (Basel II already envisaged a regulatory approach in relation to size, degree of complexity, business model and risk profile), and was officially reaffirmed in the core principles for effective banking supervision (BCBS, 2012), but, in fact, until now it has been widely disregarded except in the case of some special legal categories of credit institutions. From a strictly literal point of view, the regulatory framework prepared by the Basel Committee is to be applied only to banks operating internationally, while, in fact, over the years, the principle of 'leveling the playing field' has extended the same regulation to all banks, often irrespective of their size, with considerable cost increases, especially for small- and medium-sized banks (FSI, 2017).

The concept of proportionality only involves an adjustment to the complexity of the rules, not necessarily a lower degree of rigor. Of course, defining a regulatory framework with these characteristics requires at least a couple of essential conditions. First, prudential rules should not weaken banks' ability to absorb losses or to cope with sudden liquidity crises, thus avoiding jeopardizing their financial stability. Furthermore, proportionality should not overprotect smaller banks from unfolding competitive market forces that promote market consolidation, leading the banking industry to higher levels of efficiency (Restoy, 2018). Unfortunately, these conditions are not applied uniformly across different European countries, resulting in competitive distortions largely determined by the higher costs proportionally borne by individual credit institutions (Boss et al., 2018). It is therefore urgent that legislative debate (on the main steps, see Sattler, 2018) takes full account of regulatory aspects and supervisory practices, or the result will be the gradual marginalization of small- (and medium-) sized banks, obliged to bear significant costs for supervisory obligations without being able to benefit from size-related economies of scale.

4.5 Dealing with Old and New Competitors: From the Brick-and-Mortar Branch to Fintech

What possible strategies could banks adopt to prevent the 'crowding out effect' from fintech? Undoubtedly, a 'wait and see' strategy is to be avoided: digital technology is not a passing fad but a new and radical way of understanding and managing daily life, including (and above all) in the financial sector. The probability of succumbing to new competitors is high.

There are at least three approaches to massive integration of technology in the field of banking: an in-house approach, partnership with a fintech or participation in a technological incubator or accelerator, or full outsourcing of those products and services characterized by high technological content and a rapid rate of innovation. In-house development of technological solutions requires specific skills, often very different from those traditionally available in banks, and a significant use of capital: this could be very difficult to achieve, especially for smaller/medium banks. A partnership with a fintech company could be a strategic choice: the goal for both would have to be a win-win collaboration. On the one hand, the bank could acquire new technology and a dedicated team, enabling it to improve its offer in the shortest possible time and thus guarantee its customers a more innovative and interactive relationship, with lower costs. On the other hand, the fintech company could gain easier access to funding for continuous development of digital technology and a better reputation, thanks to a brand name and the regulation that characterize banking activity, as well as the level of trust that customers have in credit institutions (Fig. 4.3). A solution of this kind, that among practitioners appears to be the most plausible one (CapGemini et al., 2018), could also make it possible to move from product focus to customer focus, thus reducing the gap between what today's banks offer through their services and what customers actually want.

Finally, the solution involving complete outsourcing of technological innovations toward specialized players is an alternative often adopted by smaller banks with limited resources. A situation of this kind can have positive results in terms of cost efficiency, due to the scale economies

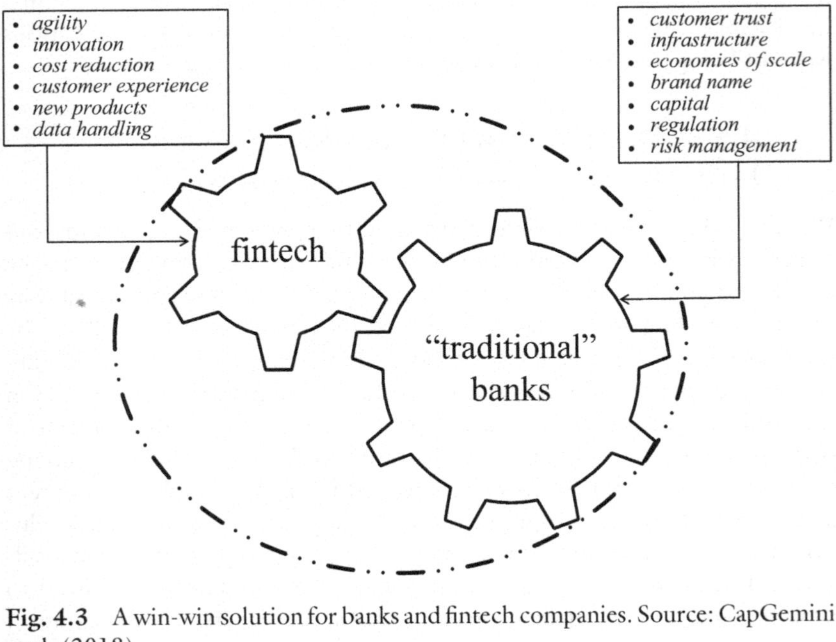

Fig. 4.3 A win-win solution for banks and fintech companies. Source: CapGemini et al. (2018)

achieved by fintech operators, but it could also generate numerous risks, even at a systemic level, in the case of default by a technology provider within a monopolistic or oligopolistic framework (Nicoletti, 2017).

Recovering efficiency and reducing total brokerage costs should be the objectives pursued by credit institutions when choosing fintech solutions, in order to ensure significant recovery in levels of profitability. Recent studies (Phillipon, 2017; Bazot, 2018) have shown that despite innovations, especially in recent decades, and despite the increasingly pervasive use of technology in banking, the unit cost of financial intermediation (obtained by dividing the income of the finance industry by the quantity of intermediated assets) has never been reduced, remaining at around 2%. The recovery of high levels of productivity does not seem to be one of the most important priorities in the strategic choices linked to digital innovation, which are instead improvement in customer experience (increased access channels, improvement in quality of services) and containment of total costs (McKinsey, 2017).

The fintech phenomenon therefore obliges intermediaries to redefine banking, in accordance with new operational logics and different organizational and governance paradigms, in anticipation of large-scale entry by the BigTech companies into the financial field. These can take advantage of recent legislative changes (possibility of being third parties in payment services, as provided for by Payment Services Directive 2 (PSD2)) and the enormous amount of data at their disposal, and they can replace traditional financial operators, offering payment and/or financing services directly to their customers.

However, it should not be forgotten that alongside the new opportunities opening up for the financial system, financial technology also brings with it numerous risks which, if amplified, can generate situations of systemic crisis. For some years now, the G-7 has recognized the pervasiveness of cyber risk and the need for sustained efforts to enhance cybersecurity in the financial sector, promoting effective practices within private and public entities and the financial sector. "Increasing in sophistication, frequency, and persistence, cyber risks are growing more dangerous and diverse, threatening to disrupt our interconnected global financial systems and the institutions that operate and support those systems. To address these risks, … high-level fundamental elements are designed for financial sector private and public entities to tailor their specific operational and threat landscape, role in the sector, and legal and regulatory requirements" (G7 Cyber Expert Group, 2016).

There are two main challenges facing regulators: first, it should be remembered that while fintech activity is by its nature global, "regulation is overseen within national or sub-national borders. This may create challenges in terms of regulatory consistency, as well as cross-border supervision and enforcement. It also creates a potential risk of regulatory arbitrage. The global nature of fintech may contribute to challenges that may be addressed by international cooperation and the exchange of information among regulators" (IOSCO, 2017). The second, and perhaps even more challenging issue, is that of leveling the playing field: regulation should be concerned with the service provided, rather than with who is providing it. It is true that in many cases, regulation and supervision are geared toward institutions, especially banks, rather than activities or services, because banks may fail, with systemic consequences. However, there is a need to find the right balance between close monitoring of the regulatory perimeter and the right neutrality in regulatory and supervisory approaches to new technology applied by incumbent institutions and other fintech firms. For these reasons, some regulators have introduced regulatory sandboxes for fintech, where companies can test innovative technologies in a live market scenario, with a degree of regulatory flexibility (EBA, 2018b; EBF, 2018; DLA Piper, 2018).

Scholars' opinions on the position that regulators should assume are not always the same: on the one hand, there are those who believe that excessive regulation can block the innovative process initiated by digital technology (Phillipon, 2017) and even prevent the development and growth of the economic system in general (Levine, 2017); on the other hand, some argue that an excessively light approach to the regulation of fintech may lead banks to exploit opportunities of regulatory arbitrage and increase the riskiness of their activities due to competitive pressure from fintechs (Bofondi and Gobbi, 2017).

4.6 Conclusions

Nowadays, banks are called on to carry out their activities in a very unstable geopolitical scenario, among new and aggressive competitors; this must be done profitably, to avoid being gradually eliminated from the market. Of course, an economic environment characterized by low interest rates and widespread severe political uncertainty does not help credit institutions to outline long-term strategies clearly. Even regulation has been perceived for a long time as a threat (and to a large extent still is), rather than an opportunity for undertaking new lines of development and experimenting with practical solutions that are different from those of the (even recent) past. Furthermore, risk is taking on a new character and different forms (cyber risk and data security) and originates from parties external to, but side by side with, the banking system itself (shadow banking and fintech).

Undoubtedly, the interaction of these factors may increase banks' vulnerability; nevertheless, a capacity for rapid reaction and a proactive approach to the management of new scenarios provide banks with the opportunity to draw up and put in place ambitious projects of transformation, above all as regards governance, organizational structures and operations. The alternative: a 'wait and see' approach or, even worse, a reluctant facing of inevitable changes, may have consequences that in the medium to long term could be fatal. The most recent attitude of the regulators seems to be oriented toward a climate of greater collaboration with banking companies; the creation of a 'testing' environment where new technologies and business models can be experimented with and developed while interacting with the regulators themselves, may prove to be not only a useful learning process for all stakeholders, but also a fundamental tool for promoting technological innovation and guaranteeing an adequate level of competition.

References

Altunbas Y., Manganelli S., Marquez-Ibanez D. (2011), Bank risk during the financial crisis: do business models matter?, ECB Working Paper Series No. 1394, November.

Ayadi R. (2019), Banking Business Models. Definition, Analytical Framework and Financial Stability Assessment, Palgrave Macmillan.

Ayadi R., Arbak E., De Groen W.P. (2011), Business Models in European Banking. A pre-and-post-crisis screening, Centre for European Policy Studies, Brussels.

Ayadi R., Arbak E., De Groen W.P. (2012), Regulation of European banks and business models: Toward a new paradigm?, Centre for European Policy Studies, Brussels.

Ayadi R., De Groen W.P., Sassi I., Mathlouthi W., Rey H., Aubry O. (2016), Banking Business Models Monitor 2015: Europe, International Research Centre on Cooperative Finance, Montréal.

Bazot G. (2018), Financial Consumption and the Cost of Finance: Measuring Financial Efficiency in Europe (1950–2007), Journal of the European Economic Association, Volume 16, issue 1, February.

BCBS – Basel Committee on Banking Supervision (2012), Core Principles for Effective Banking Supervision, September.

BCBS – Basel Committee on Banking Supervision (2017), High-level summary of Basel III reforms, December.

Bofondi M., Gobbi G. (2017), The Big Promise of FinTech, in "FinTech and Banking. Friends or Foes?", European Economy. Banks, Regulation, and the Real Sector, n. 2.

Bonaccorsi di Patti E., Palazzo F. (2018), Bank profitability and macroeconomic conditions: are business models different?, Bank of Italy, Occasional Papers no. 436, June.

Bonaccorsi di Patti E., Felici R., Signoretti F.M. (2016), Euro area significant banks: main differences and recent performance, Bank of Italy, Occasional Papers no. 306, January.

Boss M., Lederer G., Mujic N., Schwaiger M. (2018), Proportionality in banking regulation, Monetary Policy & The Economy, Oesterreichische Nationalbank, Q2/18.

CapGemini, LinkeIn, Efma (2018), World FinTech Report.

CGFS – Committee on the Global Financial System (2018), Structural changes in banking after the crisis, CGFS Papers No. 60, January.

Coen B. (2016), The global financial crisis and the future of international standard setting: lessons from the Basel Committee, Presentation given at Harvard Law School, Cambridge, MA, 12 December.

Cosma S., Ferretti R., Gualandri E., Landi A., Venturelli V. (2017), The Business Model of Banks: A Review of the Theoretical and Empirical Literature, in Chesini G., Giaretta E., Paltrinieri A. (eds), The Business of Banking. Models, Risk and Regulation, Palgrave Macmillan.

CPMI – Committee on Payments and Market Infrastructures (2014), Non-banks in retail payments, Bank for International Settlements, September.

Cunliffe J. (2017), Ten years on: Lessons from Northern Rock, Single Resolution Board Annual Conference, Brussels.

De Meo E., De Nicola A., Lusignani G., Orsini F., Zicchino L. (2016), European Banks in the XXI Century: Are Their Business Models Sustainable?, 5th EBA Policy Research Workshop "Competition in banking: implications for financial regulation and supervision", 28–29 November.

Deloitte (2018), Leading in times of change, Banking regulatory outlook 2019 – United States, December.

Di Antonio M. (2018), Business models analysis: the pitfalls of the financial data-driven approach, Bancaria, January.

DLA Piper (2018), Digital Transformation in Financial Services, October.

Draghi M. (2018), Letter to Mr. Enrique Calvet Chambon, Member of the European Parliament, 8 February.

EBA – European Banking Authority (2014), Guidelines on common procedures and methodologies for the supervisory review and evaluation process (SREP), 19 December.
EBA – European Banking Authority (2017), Risk Assessment on the European Banking System, November.
EBA – European Banking Authority (2018a), Risk Assessment on the European Banking System, December.
EBA – European Banking Authority (2018b), The EBA's Fintech Roadmap. Conclusions from the Consultation on the EBA's Approach to Financial Technology (FinTech), 15 March.
EBF – European Banking Federation (2018), EBF detailed recommendations for an EU framework of experimentation, 19 December.
ECB – European Central Bank (2016), Recent trends in euro area banks' business models and implications for banking sector stability, Financial Stability Review, May.
ECB Banking Supervision (2017a), Guidance to banks on non-performing loans, March.
ECB Banking Supervision (2017b), SSM supervisory priorities 2018, 18 December.
ECB Banking Supervision (2017c), 2017 SREP for 2018–2018 Supervisory Priorities – 2018 Stress tests, Frankfurt 18 December.
ECB Banking Supervision (2018), Addendum to the ECB Guidance to banks on non-performing loans: supervisory expectations for prudential provisioning of non-performing exposures, March.
ECB Banking Supervision (2019), Recommendation of the European Central Bank on dividend distribution policies (ECB/2019/1), 7 January.
Elliehausen G. (1998), The Cost of Bank Regulation: A Review of the Evidence, Board of Governors of the Federal Reserve System, Washington, April.
EU Commission (2018), Third Progress Report on the reduction of non-performing loans and further risk reduction in the Banking Union, Communication from the Commission to the European Parliament, the European Council and the European Central Bank, Brussels, 28 November, COM(2018) 766 final.
EU Council (2018), Non-performing loans: political agreement reached on capital requirements for banks' bad loans, 18 December, press release 815/18.
Farkas A. (2018), EU banks' business models – Adapt to thrive, Deutsche Bundesbank Conference "Bank business models – Structural changes and their systemic implications", Frankfurt, 20 February.
Feng G., Wang C. (2018), Why European banks are less profitable than U.S. banks: A decomposition approach, Journal of Banking and Finance 90 (2018), 1–16.
FSA – Financial Services Authority (2009), The Turner Review. A regulatory response to the global banking crisis, March.

FSI – Financial Stability Institute (2017), Proportionality in banking regulation: a cross-country comparison, FSI Insights on policy implementation, Bank of International Settlements, No. 1, August.

G7 Cyber Expert Group (2016), Fundamental Elements of Cybersecurity in the Financial Sector, press release, October.

Haldane A. (2009), Rethinking the Financial Network, Speech at the Financial Student Association, Amsterdam, 28 April.

Hildebrand P. (2018), What next for banking union?, Bruegel, Brussels, 8 June.

Huljak I., Mikkonen K., Moré C., Perales C. (2018), Digitalisation and its impact on banks' profitability, Box A, Financial Stability Review, November.

IMF – International Monetary Fund (2016), Global Financial Stability Report. Fostering Stability in a Low-Growth, Low-Rate Era, October.

IMF – International Monetary Fund (2017), Global Financial Stability Report. Getting The Policy Mix Right, April.

Ingves S. (2014), Implementing the regulatory reform agenda – the pitfall of myopia, Speech at the Federal Reserve Bank of Chicago Annual International Banking Conference, Chicago, 6 November.

IOSCO – International Organization of Securities Commissions (2017), Research Report on Financial Technologies (Fintech), February.

KPMG (2016), The profitability of EU banks. Hard work or a lost cause?, October.

Levine R. (2017), Comments in Phillipon T. (2017), The FinTech Opportunity, BIS Working Papers No. 655, August.

Liikanen E. (2012), High-level Expert Group on Reforming the Structure of the EU Banking Sector, Final Report, October.

Llewellyn D.T. (2013), Fifty Years in the Evolution of Bank Business Models, in Balling, M. – Gnan E. (eds.), 50 Years of Money and Finance – Lessons and Challenges, Larcier for SUERF – The European Money and Finance Forum.

McKinsey (2017), The case for digital reinvention, Digital McKinsey Survey, February.

Molyneux P. (2013), Performance in European Banking: Productivity, Profitability and Employment Trends, in Balling, M. – Gnan E. (eds.), 50 Years of Money and Finance – Lessons and Challenges, Larcier for SUERF – The European Money and Finance Forum.

Moody's (2018), Minimising cost of regulatory compliance through RegTech, September.

Nicoletti B. (2017), The future of FinTech. Integrating Finance and Technology in Financial Services, Palgrave Macmillan.

Nouy D. (2017), Too much of a good thing? The need for consolidation in the European banking sector, Speech at the VIII Financial Forum, Madrid, 27 September.

Pasiouras F., Tanna S., Zoponnidis C. (2009), The Impact of Banking Regulation on Banks' Costs and Profit Efficiency: Cross-Country Evidence, International Review of Financial Analysis, 18 (5): 294–302, December.

Phillipon T. (2017), The FinTech Opportunity, BIS Working Papers No. 655, August.
PRA – Prudential Regulation Authority (2018), Business Plan 2018/19, Bank of England.
Restoy F. (2018), Proportionality in banking regulation, speech at Westminster Business Forum Keynote Seminar "Building a resilient UK financial sector – next steps for prudential regulation, structural reform and mitigation risks, London, 4 July.
Roengpitya R., Tarashev N., Tsatsaronis K. (2014), Bank business models, BIS Quarterly Review, December.
Sattler A. (2018), Proportionality in European Banking Regulation, presentation at Policy Research Meeting on Financial Markets and Institutions, Bank of Italy, Rome, 4 October.
Schmitz M., Tirpak M. (2017), Cross-border banking in the euro area since the crisis: what is driving the great retrenchment?, Special features B, Financial Stability Review, November.
Siciliani P. (2018), Competition for retail deposits between commercial banks and non-bank operators: a two-sided platform analysis, Bank of England Staff Working Paper No. 728.
UBS (2018), The urge to merge: Consolidation to come, European Banks, Global Research, 3 September.

Final Remarks

More than fifty years ago Bob Dylan wrote that "the times they are a-changin". Those words well summarize the situation in which the banking system finds itself today, and the changes it faces. As was true then for a society exhibiting many signs of irreversible change, today too in the financial field, there are many risks and uncertainties that credit institutions have to face: an uncertain macroeconomic framework, made even more problematic by the decreased reliability of traditional forecasting indicators; a prolonged period of minimum-level interest rates (when not equal to zero, as in the case of the European Union) and abundant liquidity that could potentially have serious repercussions on the economic system; the as-yet unclearly defined role of the emerging economies which, after years of impetuous growth, have begun to slow down, with consequences still to be assessed in their current manifestation; the emergence of new risks, to a large extent related to the technological field and to the use (or rather, the misuse) of the so-called 'big data'. That facing bankers today is no easy challenge, involving as it does a plurality of actors, the interference of many exogenous factors and a different conception of what 'banking' means; moreover, despite the many rigorous studies in the field, there is no univocal empirical evidence to argue that 'one size fits all'.

Large and small banks, with different business models and with a more or less relevant role in the financial system, must coexist with new non-bank competitors (the so-called fintechs) which, at least for the time being, have

M. Borroni, S. Rossi, *Banking in Europe*, Palgrave Macmillan Studies in Banking and Financial Institutions,
https://doi.org/10.1007/978-3-030-15013-6

a formidable economic advantage due to regulatory disparity. Customers are rapidly changing their approach to the financial world, especially in the retail sector: no longer able to perceive the real added value of the service, they assume a more 'liquid behavior'—to use Zygmunt Bauman's words—and are 'unfaithful' to their bank in the search for a product or service that guarantees the lowest price for the same quality, as for any other commodity. Policymakers and supervisory authorities are struggling to identify a common regulatory framework which, while guaranteeing soundness and stability, does not harness the financial system to damaging competitive constraints. The decision-making of the 'players' in the financial world is made even more complex by the tensions of a political nature that are emerging, more or less evidently, in different countries of the old continent, and which inevitably have an effect on the uncertain development of the real economy; for the euro area countries, this is made even more fraught by the incompleteness of the Banking Union.

Collecting savings and putting them to a safe and economically advantageous use: this is banking activity in a nutshell, and hitherto the uncontested domain of banks. However, developments in technology and the creation of new financial instruments have rendered the task of credit institutions much more difficult. Perhaps the new forms of funding and lending cannot (yet), in strictly normative terms, be defined 'banking activity', but they may certainly represent interesting investment opportunities for many economic players. The crowding-out effect on banks is therefore much more than a remote possibility: in many cases, as in typical transactional activities such as those linked to the payment system, it is already a formidable reality.

It is therefore necessary to level the playing field once again, but much more rapidly than in the past, to avoid any kind of reverse discrimination toward credit institutions. Perhaps the rules governing certain activities (especially those related to payment tools) need rethinking: regulation based on the activity itself, not on who carries it out. Important changes must also take place as regards supervision, given that the systemic importance of banks is unquestionable and careful monitoring of their activity is necessary, but these are certainly not easy to implement. However, if banking activity is progressively 'taken away' from banks by other operators, it will be necessary to find suitable supervisory tools for them as well.

In some way, it is also necessary to reconcile the relationship between supervisor and supervised: the continual and urgent demands, sometimes 'imperfect and sudden' that have successively been introduced in recent years have created a relationship of respectful obedience, but often also of ill-concealed tolerance. Rules must be seen by banks as an opportunity for improving strength and growth, and not as a threat to their existence; real compliance helps improve a bank's relationship not only with the regulator but also, and above all, with its customers, dispelling any doubts about the solidity of the bank itself.

Large or small, commercial or investment, retail or wholesale, there is no one best dimension, nor a single business model, for the bank. A large size can make it easier to find capital to meet regulatory requirements and make the investments needed to respond to increasing competitive pressures. Size can help achieve better results in terms of economies of scale; it can be useful to ensure systemic importance and the status of 'too big to fail'; however, it does not necessarily guarantee a profitable activity. Even though diversification (of income revenues, geographical scope, etc.) may be a strategy to follow to enhance banks' revenue-generating capacities, it paves the way for new risks, which banks may not be aware of or be able to cope with adequately.

Perhaps it is necessary to rethink the very concept of profit, not so much in the accounting sense (it will always be the difference between costs and revenues), as much as in terms of measurement and long-term sustainability. As we have seen, on this topic, the debate is still open. Above all, in the light of the current uncertain macroeconomic context, market expectations will have to be revised, and not remain focused on profitability at pre-crisis levels.

Banks need to generate profits to maintain capital levels during unfavorable economic cycles, when higher provisioning burdens significantly reduce economic performance, while supporting the investment necessary for the development of their business and meeting increasingly stringent regulatory requirements in the field of own funds. Last but not least, they have to be able to pay dividends to their shareholders.

There is no magic wand for obtaining sustainable profits in the long term. Some bankers may have found one, but at the expense of behavioral and ethical norms, in certain cases with disastrous effects of a systemic nature. In the real world, there only remains one long and arduous search: a quest (*sic*) for profitability.

Index

M. Borroni, S. Rossi, *Banking in Europe*, Palgrave Macmillan Studies in Banking and Financial Institutions,
https://doi.org/10.1007/978-3-030-15013-6

S

The manufacturer's authorised representative in the EU is Springer Nature Customer Service Centre GmbH, Europaplatz 3, 69115 Heidelberg, Germany. If you have any concerns regarding our products, please contact ProductSafety@springernature.com

Printed and bound by CPI Group (UK) Ltd, Croydon, CR0 4YY
25/09/2026
02222890-0012